D1458224

Spared *by* Grace

An Inspiring True Story of Miracles and Answered Prayers

John C. Buchan

WESTBOW
P R E S S®
A DIVISION OF THOMAS NELSON
& ZONDERVAN

WestBow Press books may be ordered through booksellers or by contacting:

WestBow Press
A Division of Thomas Nelson & Zondervan
1663 Liberty Drive
Bloomington, IN 47403
www.westbowpress.com
1 (866) 928-1240

ISBN: 978-1-9736-6442-0 (sc)
ISBN: 978-1-9736-6443-7 (hc)
ISBN: 978-1-9736-6441-3 (e)

Library of Congress Control Number: 2019907184

Print information available on the last page.

WestBow Press rev. date: 06/17/2019

A wife of noble character who can find?
She is worth far more than rubies.
Her husband has full confidence in her and lacks nothing of value.
She brings him good, not harm, all the days of her life.

—Proverbs 31:10–12 (NIV)

Spared by Grace is dedicated to Frances, my wonderful
wife and best friend; to my very dear children; and
the many faithful people who prayed for me.

Contents

Acknowledgments

I am deeply grateful to everyone who encouraged me to write this book, particularly my wife and family. Many details would have been impossible to document without their help and guidance.

I also thank David McCaig, who serves Peterhead Baptist Church as pastor. His initial request that I share my testimony and the subsequent encouragement I've received contributed to *Spared by Grace*.

Special mention must be made of my nephew's wife, Sheilann Wilson. A fresh pair of eyes to proofread the manuscript, pointing out any areas that needed more explanation, was appreciated. I'm sure her assistance has lightened the load for WestBow Press, whom I would also like to thank; this would not have been completed without their guidance.

In addition, special recognition must be given to the National Health Service (NHS), in particular the medical staff who cared for me, for their many skills, gifts, patience, and dedication.

Above all else, most sincere thanks go to our gracious God and loving Heavenly Father. Without the many miracles and answered prayers that have been bestowed on me, I would not be alive to share my story. I pray this humble effort will be both pleasing to him and a blessing to many.

Amen

Introduction

Give thanks to the Lord, call on his name,
make known among the nations what he has done.
—Psalm 105:1 (NIV)

I left home for work on a beautiful summer's morning. The next thing I remember was four weeks later: I was in a hospital and had suffered catastrophic, life-threatening injuries.

It was a miracle I was alive.

This is my story.

chapter 1

Beginnings

It is God who arms me with strength and keeps my way secure.
—2 Samuel 22:33 (NIV)

WHO WOULD HAVE imagined that a simple fisherman such as I from the northeast of Scotland would ever write a book? However, God had a plan and has given me a remarkable story to tell, and I feel compelled to share it. My hope is that everyone who reads this will be strengthened and encouraged by it.

I was born on May 30, 1966, to the late John and Barbara Buchan. I grew up with my older sister, Grace, in Peterhead, a small coastal fishing town in the northeast of Scotland. I had a great childhood and have many happy memories. I was fortunate and privileged to be brought up in a loving Christian home where church life was always important. I regularly attended Sunday school as a youngster, although I don't remember enjoying it much. Looking back now, I think I probably always believed in the existence of God, but other than that acknowledgment, I didn't spare him much thought.

I did reasonably well at school and gained my qualifications before leaving, but I didn't have much interest in academics. All I wanted to do was go to sea. I left school as soon as possible at the age of sixteen and went to work as a fisherman on the family boat. This was a great career, and I very much enjoyed the excitement and challenges this new way of life brought. Long hours of arduous physical work were often required, sometimes in tough winter conditions. Despite this, fishing can also be both satisfying and rewarding. Once I had gained the necessary experience, skills, and qualifications, I progressed to skipper of the boat when my father retired in 1992. This new role brought many challenges and responsibilities as the safety of the crew, along with the viability of the vessel, rested mainly with the skipper. Having said that, I also felt a deep sense of satisfaction each time a good catch was made. I'm sure this must have been driven by competitiveness, as I don't remember financial gain being the main motivation. Nevertheless, the crew's wages were based on a share of the catch, and no fish meant no pay. Many years ago, there was a television documentary about the fishing industry entitled *Last of the Hunters*. The title is probably a fair description of fishermen and the way the boats are operated.

I first met my wife, Frances, when I was twenty years old, and as we started dating, I settled down somewhat and began accompanying her to Peterhead Baptist Church. It's very likely this was to please Frances initially, but I soon began to look forward to and enjoy attending church on Sundays when I was at home. I can't remember the exact date I gave my life to the Lord, but I do remember the message that was preached that night from Matthew 7:13–14. As Jesus began his summary of the Sermon on the Mount, he said,

> Heaven can be entered only through the narrow gate! The highway to hell is broad, and its gate is wide enough for all the multitudes who choose its easy way. But the Gateway to Life is small, and the road is narrow, and only a few ever find it. (TLB)

The pastor explained in more detail about the wide and narrow roads, and no matter what anyone thought, they were traveling on one or the other; there was no such thing as middle ground. I felt he was speaking directly to me as I saw myself on the fence. I was convicted of my sin that night and asked the Lord for his forgiveness and for him to come into my heart. I was saved!

Many years have passed since that night, and time seems to have flown by. Frances and I were married on September 22, 1989, in Peterhead. I was a partner in a successful fishing business that grew and expanded over the years. I was very happily married to a beautiful wife, and in due course, we had three wonderful children: Stephanie, Shannon, and John. I have indeed always felt very privileged. A range of different fishing opportunities took the vessel all around the coast of the United Kingdom, with the result that the boat was frequently at sea over the weekend. Seasonal opportunities, available quotas of fish to catch, and weather conditions all contributed to how long we spent away from home, which could occasionally be up to a month at any one time. This may sound quite tough, but we were used to it, and the days spent at home between fishing trips were generally free and always great fun. When my children were young, they likened it to being on holiday every time I was home.

Since being saved, my faith has been always important in my life, but so were many other things, although I still enjoyed attending church and hearing God's Word being shared when I was at home. Having said that, I'm sure I never really put God first and gave him his rightful place in my life.

I rededicated my life to the Lord during one weekend many years ago. I was challenged when an American evangelist was speaking in Peterhead. I can't give you the date, but I felt my faith had slipped.

chapter 2

Close Calls, Difficulties,
and Challenges

For I am convinced that neither death nor life, neither angels nor
demons, neither the present nor the future, nor any powers, neither
height nor depth, nor anything else in all creation, will be able to
separate us from the love of God that is in Christ Jesus our Lord.

—Romans 8:38–39 (NIV)

So do not fear, for I am with you; do not be dismayed,
for I am your God. I will strengthen you and help you;
I will uphold you with my righteous right hand.

—Isaiah 41:10 (NIV)

Malta

THE YEAR AFTER Frances and I were married, 1990, we were on
holiday on the Mediterranean island of Malta. The hotel we stayed in
was located in a beautiful bay on the north coast of the island. One of
the many activities available at the resort was parasailing, which was
very popular. It entailed a short flight around the bay while suspended
from a parachute in the beautiful Mediterranean weather and was
great fun. On one particular occasion, Frances had just returned, and

it was my turn to go up. While I was getting into the harness and the chute was being prepared, the light breeze completely dropped. To compensate, more power was used on the powerboat to fill the parachute with air and enable lift. When I eventually reached the maximum altitude, the towline snapped about two meters in front of me, the line whipped back across my face, and I swiftly fell into the sea, landing a few meters from the rocks. To me, this all seemed to happen very quickly. Inevitably, much panic followed as the hotel staff rushed to the scene to free me from the parachute, which had landed on top of me. Amazingly, I was fine and suffered no more serious injuries than whiplash and a few minor cuts and bruises. Ironically, I was offered a free flight as compensation. Needless to say, I declined! Many times, people remarked that I was lucky not to have sustained far more serious injuries.

Shetland

Two years later, as we were coming to the end of a fishing trip in the North Sea, the trawl was being recovered for the last time before the vessel returned to Peterhead. My hand was accidentally caught in a rope and crushed. The vessel quickly proceeded to a port in the nearby Shetland Islands so I could go to the local hospital and have my injured hand checked. The superintendent from the local Fishermen's Mission met us on the quayside and drove my father and me to casualty, a distance of approximately six miles. Following an examination, the doctor was quite sure I had fractured a small bone in my hand. Due to the fact we were on our way home to the mainland anyway, he was satisfied to discharge me with the stipulation that I would go to the hospital in Peterhead on arrival for x-rays. My hand was bandaged, my arm was put in a sling, and we were sent on our way.

On the return journey to the boat, we ran into black ice on the road. The driver lost control and the car skidded, hit the verge, and rolled over, coming to a stop on its roof in a ditch by the side of the road. It felt as if I had been thrown about like a ball in the backseat, but—despite wearing no seatbelt and having one arm in a sling—I was unharmed. No one in the car suffered more than minor cuts and bruises. Given the fact there were no mobile phones or any other means of communication, we walked the remaining two miles back to the boat. Again, it was said we were very lucky! Imagine the surprised look on Frances's face when I returned home to Peterhead following a week at sea and tried to explain how I'd been involved in a car crash!

English Channel

In January 1997, fishing opportunities brought us to the western English Channel; this was a normal part of our annual fisheries program and something we had done for many years. We sailed on January 11 from the small port of Weymouth following the annual Christmas and New Year break at home—our first trip of the year. A few shoals of fish were detected by sonar, and fishing operations commenced for a couple of hours that afternoon. Upon completion, the catch of pilchards was taken aboard by one of our partner vessels, and the search for more shoals began again. This was typical for this type of fishery and the search continued throughout the night, but to no avail as no further shoals were found. At around four thirty in the morning, two crewmen were called to the wheelhouse and the watch was set, and I went to bed for a couple of hours as we slowly returned to the area where the fish had been detected the previous afternoon. I was rudely awoken shortly afterward by shouting and obvious panic from the watchmen in the wheelhouse, and I discovered a large cargo vessel had collided with us. I described this in a statement I made afterward as the most terrifying experience of my life. The bulk carrier had ploughed into us in dense fog, when the visibility at the time was approximately fifty to one hundred meters (164 to 328 feet).

Marine accident investigators concluded that, upon impact, our fishing vessel must have heeled over to a very alarming sixty or seventy degrees. The bulk carrier had rammed into us directly on the strongest part of the vessel, this being the steel bulkhead between the engine room and the fish hold. Had the impact been one or two meters on either side of this, it is very likely that the steel hull would have ruptured significantly, and the vessel may have quickly foundered. Bearing in mind the dense fog, abandoning ship and taking to a life raft in busy shipping lanes was not a favorable prospect. The crew checked the vessel and found seawater in several compartments. We issued a Mayday, and a number of nearby vessels immediately offered assistance. Fortunately, this wasn't required as the bilge-pumping system could handle the water ingress, meaning the vessel was able to struggle to port on her own, escorted by our partner fishing vessel and the local lifeboat. Once the initial panic and confusion settled down and we were slowly making our way to harbor, I clearly remember remarking to the crew, "We have no one to thank but the Lord for being alive." This was very real to me at the time, but I never spoke about it much.

Upon our safe arrival in port, we were met by many people, including insurance company representatives, marine surveyors, maritime and coast guard agency investigators, and shipyard personnel. The focus turned swiftly to the cause of the accident and to getting the boat repairs underway as soon as possible. The headline in the *Fishing News* the following week read, "Miracle Escape for Pair Trawler Crew." I fully appreciate this was a press release and the term *miracle* is often used out of context—I suspect when there is no clear explanation found for a positive outcome. I'll leave you to make up your own mind. I fully knew God's hand was in this. No one was injured; none of the crew even sustained as much as a scratch. Maybe not so surprisingly now, but it was said many times that we had been "lucky." After I phoned to inform Frances of the whole drama and reassure her that everyone was safe, she went to open her Bible to read Psalm 23. She says the following verse just seemed to jump out of the page at her, and this has been a favorite verse of ours ever since.

> The Lord reached down from above and took hold of me; he pulled me out of the deep waters. (Psalm 18:16 GNT)

These truly were amazing words.

Frances remembers sitting at home on New Year's Eve a couple of weeks prior to this whole incident, reflecting on how good a year we'd had and all the things we had planned for the upcoming year without thanking God or even considering him. She also remembers praying after first hearing about the collision, "God, you didn't have to do this to get our attention," and then realizing that perhaps he did. Substantial repairs to the vessel got underway and were completed in record time, and although maritime investigations continued and the responsible vessel was eventually found, we were back fishing two months after the collision and life seemed to return to normal.

Peterhead Harbour

On a beautiful day the following summer (1998), while the vessel's crew discharged the day's catch of fresh herring into trucks, I proceeded to make my way ashore to speak with the fish processors and Frances, who were on the quayside. Peterhead Harbour has a large tidal range of several meters, and as it was low tide at the time, I went to step from the boat onto the steel access ladder. These are normally built into the quayside wall to enable access to and from vessels at low tide and are used every day. When I stepped across, my foot slipped. and I fell between the vessel and the quayside into the water—probably a height of three to four meters and an approximate width of around one meter. Before I knew anything, I was in the harbor. Fortunately, I surfaced beside the ladder and was able to climb up. To fall through such a narrow gap without touching either the steel vessel or the concrete wall of the quay was remarkable. I could very easily have been knocked unconscious. None of the crew or bystanders knew anything untoward had taken place until I appeared at the top of the ladder and climbed onto the quayside soaking wet. It was another drama, but at least it provided a good subject at school the following week for my five-year-old daughter Stephanie's show and tell.

Sparkling Star sold—the end of an era for my family

The business slowly grew and expanded over the next few years. Nevertheless, fishing regulations became more onerous, and as licensing and restrictions on fishing activity became more challenging, the prospects for the future were uncertain. The available quota to catch was reduced, and the opportunity to purchase more quickly went beyond our financial reach. Despite very much enjoying the career and way of life, we made the tough decision to sell the business as a whole and stopped fishing in 2003. There had been a fishing boat in my family for over a hundred years; this was therefore a big decision to make and would be a significant change for everyone to adapt to.

I soon found myself employed as a fishing industry representative on a number of research vessels operating mainly in the North Sea; these were primarily involved in the offshore oil and gas industry. This was followed by three years as master on a Scottish government oceanographic and fisheries research vessel based in Aberdeen, another very interesting part of my career. Finally in 2011, a suitable opportunity became available to work ashore, and I was employed as director of marine operations for the commercial arm of the Scottish Fisherman's Federation (SFF Services). This oil and gas industry service company is based in Aberdeen, and the experience I gained over the previous few years was to serve me well in my new role.

SFF Services provided personnel and fishing vessels to the offshore oil and gas industry, which were chartered or contracted to assist with specific offshore projects. Initially, my job consisted mostly of inspecting a range of fishing vessels to ensure they met the rigorous standards of the industry. It was also my responsibility to brief both skippers and crews on the details and instructions of the relevant project. The work was very busy and frequently demanding, but I did enjoy the challenges of meeting the variety of people involved in both industries. Initially, I traveled throughout Scotland to various ports in order to conduct these inspections, and later I was based full-time in the Aberdeen office.

Working in an office every day was something I never would have foreseen or expected; it was just not my cup of tea. The job was fast paced and demanding, and I received over a hundred emails every day. Replying to these along with attending various project and planning meetings and reading, editing, and writing numerous reports was time consuming and mentally challenging. This was all new to me and took some time to get used to, but I seemed to adapt well and eventually settled in fine. Who can predict the often unexpected and unusual paths that life will present? These skills and experiences were invaluable and have helped greatly when writing *Spared by Grace*, which would have been almost impossible before I worked in the Aberdeen office.

> "For I know the plans I have for you," declares the Lord, "plans to prosper you and not to harm you, plans to give you hope and a future." (Jeremiah 29:11 NIV)

*Happy times: my family celebrated my dad's eightieth birthday
on New Year's Eve 2012. Everyone was looking forward to a
new year. Who could have known what it would hold?*

2013: A Difficult Year

The year 2013 began with the sad and sudden passing of my sister's
husband, Alex, at the age of fifty-five in January. Following a short
illness, he was admitted to Aberdeen Royal Infirmary for planned
routine surgery. A number of complications developed, and Alex was
moved to the intensive care unit. His condition further deteriorated,
and twelve days later he sadly passed away during emergency surgery.
I was at the office in Aberdeen when I received the message that Alex
had been taken for an emergency operation, and I went straight to
the hospital to keep my sister Grace and her family company as they
anxiously awaited results. This was a very tragic time for us all, but
in particular for my sister and her family. Alex was a Christian man
who had given his life to the Lord many years earlier; nevertheless,
circumstances like these are difficult and very tough to accept. We do,
however, have great comfort and hope in the assurance that Alex is
now at peace with the Lord, although the sadness and loss is still very
evident in his family.

My mother also passed away later the same year. Her fatal illness began in July when she broke a bone in her arm and a serious infection subsequently developed. She was admitted to the orthopedic unit at Aberdeen Royal Infirmary, but despite every effort to treat the infection, it spread to the many metal replacement joints in her body. These had been fitted gradually over many years as she suffered from osteoarthritis. Her consultant had previously warned us of this potential risk, and when the infection did reach the metalwork, it was beyond treatment. She held onto life for nine days after the night we were advised the doctors didn't expect her to last until morning and that there was no more they could do. Those nine days proved to be extremely difficult and a huge trial for everyone, but my father and sister were particularly affected by the strain, especially as it came so soon after the shock of Alex's death.

Toward the end of the same year, I also lost an aunt and an uncle. The year of 2013 sadly ended as a year of many losses.

As surprising as it may sound, it's only on looking back and piecing together these details that I fully appreciate the extent of what God has taken my family and me through, irrespective of the many times I have let him down. Often I feel as if I have drifted far from him, but even then he has never left me and has carried me through some almost unbelievable circumstances.

> I am with you and will watch over you wherever you go, and I will bring you back to this land. I will not leave you until I have done what I have promised you. (Genesis 28:15 NIV)

chapter 3

Why Don't We See a
Peterhead Miracle?

The Lord himself goes before you and will be with
you; he will never leave you nor forsake you.
Do not be afraid; do not be discouraged.
—Deuteronomy 31: 8 (NIV)

"THE LORD WILL go before you." This is so true but isn't always apparent until after an event. I trust this chapter will clearly demonstrate how the Lord went before us as a family, preparing and strengthening us for the events that would transpire later.

At our local church in Peterhead, Frances helped out occasionally in leading a Bible study for teenagers. During Easter 2014, they looked at Jesus' resurrection and discussed how devastated the disciples were when he died. Their hopes were crushed, but God did so much more than they could ever ask or imagine (see Ephesians 3:20) when he raised Jesus from the dead and turned what seemed like a hopeless tragedy into a glorious new beginning. They spoke about the great hope there is in Jesus, how the same mighty power that raised him from the dead is at work in those who believe in him (see Ephesians 1:19–20), and how nothing is impossible for God. Even the most seemingly insurmountable problem is tiny to him, whose love reaches to the heavens and whose faithfulness stretches to the skies. They went on to speak about some of the times recounted in the Bible when God stepped in and did the impossible, the immeasurably more, such as with Moses and the Israelites at the Red Sea, when Joseph was sold as a slave to Egypt, with David and Goliath, and with Lazarus, who was raised back from death to life. They spoke about how "Jesus Christ is the same yesterday and today and forever" (Heb. 13:8 NIV) and that no matter how bad things appear to be, when you set your eyes on Jesus, he will fill you with hope. The discussion continued to more recent miracles that had occurred around Peterhead but none that had actually taken place *in* Peterhead when one girl, Olivia, asked, "Why don't we see a Peterhead miracle?"

Life at home was very busy during the following couple of months, as plans and preparations were being made for my eldest daughter's wedding. Stephanie was married to Michael Campbell on Friday, June 6, 2014. This was indeed a very happy day, and given the sadness and loss our family had experienced throughout the previous year, it was very welcome. It was a great day for family and friends to share time with one another in celebrating their wedding. People who have gone through the experience will appreciate how busy things can get in the run-up to the wedding day; many hours are required planning every detail, from guest lists and invitations to table plans and flowers, gifts, clothes, and so on. In addition, I was very busy at work, as the company I worked for was experiencing record levels of activity, and it seemed like I was struggling to find enough hours in each day. I remember spending what felt like every spare minute I had trying to prepare my "Father of the Bride" speech. This wasn't something I was completely comfortable with, as the thought of speaking in front of the wedding guests was daunting to me, but I knew how important it was to Stephanie and that it had to be done.

Stephanie and Michael's wedding day

The big event came around quickly and took place on a beautiful summer's day at an excellent hotel on the outskirts of Aberdeen. The wedding service was conducted by Mr. Alex John Strachan from Peterhead, a family acquaintance for many years, and was full of sound spiritual advice and guidance for the couple's future life together. The whole day went smoothly despite the hotel's loss of electrical power during the evening reception. Nothing could be done to resolve the situation, and the *ceilidh* (party) was put on hold for a couple of hours. The resultant candlelight provided an excellent opportunity for conversation, and the blackout didn't seem to spoil the occasion in any way. Many guests actually remarked on how much they enjoyed it. I was introduced to people from America who were visiting a church in Peterhead for a few weeks during the summer. They were friends of the groom's parents and had been given short notice—almost last-minute—invitation to the wedding, as other guests had unexpectedly declined. Having never experienced a wedding in Scotland before, they were delighted and very much enjoyed the whole occasion. A few days later they returned home to the States and soon became part of the amazing worldwide prayers that were to come. Michael and Stephanie went on honeymoon the following morning, and everyone else seemed to settle back into normal life.

Two weeks passed, and on Stephanie and Michael's return from their honeymoon, both family and friends gathered at our house on Saturday evening, where we enjoyed a barbecue and welcomed the married couple home. The newlywed's house was not quite ready to move into, so they were alternating between staying at our house and with Michael's parents, John and Michelle.

Barbecue on a Saturday evening

We have since discovered that, a few days after the wedding, Stuart Watt, a friend who serves as pastor in a village near Peterhead, had been browsing through photographs of the wedding on social media. When he saw my photograph, he felt called to pray for me. (Perhaps he was concerned about the bill I was facing!) He didn't know why, but he knew he was being led to pray for John Buchan.

Frances was scheduled to lead the Bible study again on the morning of Sunday, June 22, and as she was preparing for it, she read Acts 3:1–22 every day for two weeks, including the following verses.

> By faith in the name of Jesus, this man whom you see
> and know was made strong. It is Jesus name and the faith
> that comes through him that has given this complete
> healing to him as you can all see. (Acts 3:16 NIV)

For the man who was miraculously healed was over
40 years old.
(Acts 4:22 NIV)

God had gone before her!

On the evening of Sunday, June 22, 2014, Frances and I attended a service at the AOG Central Church in the nearby town of Fraserburgh. There had been an afternoon event at our local church in Peterhead, with the result that the evening service was canceled. We have many friends and family who regularly attend the Assembly of God church in Fraserburgh, and as we hadn't been there for several months, we thought it was an ideal opportunity to meet up. Frances remembers me saying before the service began that we wouldn't be able to stay for tea after the service, as I was going to be very busy at work the next day and would need to get home. We did, however, end up staying for tea and had a great time of fellowship, and we ended up being the last people to leave the church before they closed the doors.

Shortly after finishing work two days later, my son John Jr. and I went for a bike ride in the evening. The weather was great, and we cycled around the edge of town, along the river, past the harbor and the bay, finishing up at the local marina, a distance of roughly six miles. This was a fairly familiar route to us that we very much enjoyed and did quite often. John had recently bought a new Go-Pro camera, and after recording part of our ride, he was keen to attach the telescopic arm and attempt to film some fish underwater at the marina—all lots of good fun. It really was a beautiful, calm, and still summer evening, and we arrived home between nine thirty and ten o'clock that evening as the sun was setting. I quickly went up to an old monument tower that is located on a hilltop behind our house and provided a great vantage point from which to photograph the summer sunset.

The view turned out to be the last memory I have before my life changed forever.

John C. Buchan

Sunset at Meethill Tower, June 24, 2014

chapter 4

The Day My Life Changed Forever

Do not boast about tomorrow, for you do not
know what a day may bring forth.
—Proverbs 27:1 (NIV)

But those who suffer he delivers them in their suffering;
he speaks to them in their affliction.
—Job 36:15 (NIV)

I have been driven many times upon my knees by the overwhelming
conviction that I have nowhere else to go. My own wisdom
and that of all about me seemed insufficient for that day.
—Abraham Lincoln

THE FIRST VERSE above states, "for you do not know what a day may bring forth," and in many ways this is probably just as well. A friend once said, "It's a good thing we don't know what's ahead of us, or perhaps we wouldn't get up in the morning." On Wednesday, June 25, 2014, I left home as usual at 6:45 a.m. for the routine hour-long drive along the coast to work in Aberdeen. It was a beautiful summer morning, and I had a busy day ahead; by all accounts it seemed like a fairly normal sort of day up to that point, although Frances remembers thinking as I left the house that morning that she especially needed to pray for me that day.

At around ten minutes past eight, Frances was about to drive our son John to school when the doorbell rang. The police were at the door. The officer introduced himself and asked Frances the following question: "Is this your husband's wallet? It has forty pounds in it." He went on to explain that I had been seriously injured in a road traffic accident and airlifted to Aberdeen Royal Infirmary (ARI). He then asked if she would be able to get to the hospital.

It is difficult to comprehend or imagine the shock a statement like this must have been for Frances, and she didn't fully grasp what the officer said but has since likened its effect to going onto autopilot. She made a couple of quick phone calls to my dad and her mum and then, along with Shannon and John, set off for Aberdeen, with Michael and Stephanie following behind in their own car. Although it hadn't crossed anyone's mind, of course the road was closed due to the accident. All traffic by this time had been diverted onto narrow countryside roads, and it wasn't long before they were completely clogged with the increasing volume of traffic. Frances cried out to the Lord in her head, *Lord, please help us! Please help us get to Aberdeen!* Alex John Strachan, the gentleman who had married Stephanie and Michael only two weeks earlier, was also stuck in traffic; he was heading in the opposite direction, and as both cars came to a standstill next to each other, Frances told him what she knew about the accident and explained that they were trying to get to the hospital. He was full of apologies as he didn't know what to suggest, but Frances was thankful for meeting him nevertheless, as she knew he would pray and ask other people to pray.

> Hear my prayer, Lord; let my cry for help come to you.
> Do not hide your face from me when I am in distress.
> Turn your ear to me; when I call, answer me quickly.
> (Psalm 102:1–2 NIV)

God answered her prayer and made a way. They stopped opposite what looked like a farm entrance, and as Michael had previously lived in that area, he thought he might have some idea of where the road went. This may have seemed like a risk to take as it was a rough, single-lane road with long grass and weeds growing in the middle, but it eventually led back onto the main road, and they didn't encounter another car. Now that they were clear of the traffic and moving again, Frances began to take in what the police officer had said: "Seriously injured," "airlifted to hospital." *What did he mean?* she wondered. *Does John have a broken leg? Would that constitute a serious injury? Is it his spine or his head?* When they eventually arrived at the accident and emergency department (A&E), her heart sank even further as they were taken aside and led to a room designated for relatives.

A doctor came into the room and listed my injuries to my family: two broken femurs, a shattered left knee, a broken tibia and fibula in the left leg, a shattered right ankle, a smashed left arm, a broken right arm, internal bleeding, collapsed lung on both sides, static spinal fractures, and an orbital fracture above my right eye. Beyond that, they didn't yet know about the possibility of brain damage. He then left my family in no doubt as to how serious the situation was when he added, "I should make you aware we wouldn't normally expect someone with these injuries to make it to the hospital."

Car wreck at the accident scene (photograph by Police Scotland)

A short time later, Frances was advised that a CT scan had been performed, and there was no obvious indication of any injury to my brain. The doctor also told her she could come and see me for a moment before I was taken to the operating room. Frances was led to a treatment room where I was lying on a bed covered by a sheet up to my shoulders; she remembers there being about twelve doctors and medical staff standing around the bed. Frances put her hand on my shoulder as she spoke to me and describes me as being stone cold to touch and lifeless. At this point, she thought that I wasn't there and may have died, but she never shared this with anyone at the time. She couldn't help but think that I had either died or the doctors were sure I would and were simply being kind by letting her see my body before I went to the operating room. A short time after she returned to the relative's room, the doctor returned and gave her my wedding ring, saying, "I want you to look after this" (details to come in chapter 10). My dad and sister Grace had arrived at the hospital along with Frances's mum and sister Monica, and by this time most of them had heard how serious the accident had been and that the other driver had sadly died. This must have been an extremely difficult experience for my family—at the time my life really was hanging by a mere thread. They were all a great comfort and support for one another.

Frances read her Bible, verses such as John 11:25–26 and verse 40, which tell of the death and resurrection of Lazarus, and also Psalm 91, which promises God's help and protection in the midst of danger. Her sister Monica read the following verse out loud.

> Go back and report to John what you have seen and heard: The blind receive sight, the lame walk, those who have leprosy are cured, the deaf hear, the dead are raised and the good news is preached to the poor. (Luke 7:22 NIV)

This gave them all hope.

Car wreck (photograph by Police Scotland)

It's difficult to find the words to describe their feelings at this time, but they recall how much they felt upheld in prayer and how they appreciated receiving many text messages from people who were praying. These were all a great source of encouragement and comfort as they waited anxiously.

I went through thirteen hours of extensive surgery on that first day. The surgeries were carried out by several different medical teams, each one specializing in a particular field. Chest drains were inserted into each lung; both fractured femurs were stabilized using a combination of nails, plates, and screws; and my left tibia was similarly repaired. A laparotomy (a large abdominal incision) was also conducted to investigate and control internal bleeding. Doctors discovered a lacerated spleen and were able to glue the tear. Both forearm fractures were also immobilized in plaster, and an external fixator was fitted to my lower right leg in preparation for surgery at a later date. Throughout these procedures, I received over thirty units of blood products. When the surgeries were over, I was admitted to intensive care, where my family was allowed to see me for a few minutes. Frances says she can't explain how difficult it was to leave me that night, but she remembered this verse.

But I am a God who is everywhere and not in one place only. (Jeremiah 23:23 GNT)

When Frances arrived home and went to bed that night, she prayed "Lord is this it? Am I going to be a widow at forty-six?"

The diagnosis and list of injuries recorded in my medical notes that day are as follows:

> Severe Traumatic Brain Injury and Polytrauma due to road traffic accident on 25/06/14: bilateral femoral fractures, bilateral tibial fractures, bilateral forearm fractures, multiple right-sided rib fractures, left patella fracture, lacerated spleen, internal bleeding, orbital skull fracture, brain injury, two collapsed lungs, two static lumbar spine fractures, Glasgow Coma Scale (GCS) recorded at 5 at the scene.

chapter 5

Intensive Care and
Orthopedic Trauma Unit

The cords of death entangled me; the torrents of destruction overwhelmed me. The cords of the grave coiled around me; the snares of death confronted me. In my distress I called to the Lord; I cried to my God for help. From his temple he heard my voice; my cry came before him, into his ears.

—Psalm 18:4–6 (NIV)

I will exalt you, Lord, for you lifted me out of the depths and did not let my enemies gloat over me. Lord my God, I called to you for help, and you healed me. You, Lord, brought me out from the realm of the dead; you spared me from going down to the pit.

—Psalm 30:1–3 (NIV)

I will not die but live, and will proclaim what the Lord has done. The Lord has chastened me severely, but he has not given me over to death.

—Psalm 118:17, 18 (NIV)

AT HOME WE have done a daily reading from the devotional booklet *Our Daily Bread* for many years, and the morning after the accident, the reading was from Psalm 46 (NIV):

God is our refuge and strength, an ever-present help in trouble.

Therefore we will not fear, though the earth give way and the mountains fall into the heart of the sea, though its waters roar and foam and the mountains quake with their surging. There is a river whose streams make glad the city of God, the holy place where the Most High dwells. God is within her, she will not fall; God will help her at break of day. Nations are in uproar, kingdoms fall; he lifts his voice, the earth melts. The Lord Almighty is with us; the God of Jacob is our fortress. Come and see what the Lord has done, the desolation he has brought on the earth. He makes wars cease to the ends of the earth; he breaks the bow and shatters the spear; he burns the shields with fire. Be still and know that I am God; I will be exalted among the nations, I will be exalted in the earth. The Lord Almighty is with us; the God of Jacob is our fortress.

These were very appropriate and comforting words for my family. Frances says it felt as if their mountains had just fallen into the sea, and God really was their refuge and strength. There was nothing or no one else for them to cling to. There was no change in my situation that day; I was still in a coma. Frances remembers at some point during the day that I was bending my left knee, and the nurse at my bedside was quick to say, "Oh, he really shouldn't be able to do that." A brace was swiftly fitted to prevent me from doing this again.

The following day was Friday, June 27. A news reporter came to the door of our home holding a photograph of me walking our daughter Stephanie down the aisle on her wedding day. He said he was looking for the family of the man in the photograph and was advised to try this door. Frances quickly said, "No comment" and closed the door as she felt unable to speak to him. She was so thankful and relieved for not having been drawn in to saying something that may have been misunderstood and misreported in the local newspaper.

I was taken to surgery again, and both my forearms were further repaired using a number of titanium plates and screws. My left forearm in particular was extensively damaged and required double plating; one surgeon speaking to Frances afterward described the bones as "powder" and said he wasn't sure if or to what extent they would heal. Following these surgeries I was readmitted to intensive care, where there continued to be no change throughout the following couple of days; I remained in a coma.

Just before the end of visiting time on Sunday, June 29, while Frances was still at my bedside, the doctor came and told her I had developed a chest infection, a common complication that can result from being on a ventilator. The doctor described the type of bacteria as difficult to treat and very resistant to antibiotics. He then went on to say that if the infection reached the recently inserted metalwork, they wouldn't be able to treat it but he would keep his fingers crossed. My family was familiar with this risk, as bacteria clinging to internal metalwork had sadly resulted in my mother's death the previous year (chapter 2). Frances remembers feeling annoyed because he had said this at my bedside, and even though I was unconscious, she was sure I could hear because I had squeezed her hand. Also, crossing your fingers is no hope at all. What hope is there in crossing your fingers? This will only give you arthritis in your fingers! She prayed against infection right there at my bedside, out loud for me to hear, and then the text messages were sent "please pray against infection" to our faithful prayer warriors. Her sister Monica was always a great support to Frances and a great help in sending out the many prayer requests.

As my family was on their way home the same day, Frances received a text message from a friend at church, Fiona. It said, "We are meeting at my house to pray for John Buchan. Would you like to come?' It was almost immediately followed by another message that said, "Sorry, Frances. That wasn't meant for you." Frances replied, "Oh, yes, it was." This was just the encouragement she needed. My family was greatly heartened to know that people were taking the time to meet together to pray for me.

Initially, Frances thought she would look up the bacteria when she got home, but she didn't. Instead she remembered Peter's mother-in-law, who had been ill in bed with a fever. Jesus rebuked the fever, it left her, and she got up and served them (Luke 4:38–39).

But the advocate, the Holy Spirit, whom the Father will send in my name, will teach you all things and will remind you of everything I have said to you. (John 14:26 NIV)

Frances was also reminded of how God had kept me from infection when I was working on a boat in Egypt several years previously, which was certainly answered prayer. She knew that it didn't matter what bacteria it was—Jesus can rebuke it. It's nothing to him. He is in control of the whole universe; He spoke the world into being! She prayed about it and was encouraged and thankful to know that other people were praying too. She remembers feeling the peace of God that really passes all understanding, which is described in Philippians 4:6–7.

Another remarkable outcome! God answered those prayers, the infection didn't spread, and it cleared up completely. Despite numerous wounds and compound fractures, I didn't develop a single additional infection throughout almost six months in the hospital. On one particular occasion while in the trauma unit, the orthopedic ward experienced an outbreak of a stomach bug, and many patients were affected as well as some staff, but again I was spared. Some may claim that this is no more than good fortune or that I was lucky, but I had suffered a lacerated spleen. One of the main functions of the spleen is to help fight infection.

On another occasion my son-in-law Michael was sitting at my bedside in intensive care when all of a sudden I started to move my right leg. This was where the external fixator (a metal, cylindrical, cage-like device fixed directly to the bones so as to stabilize and immobilize them) was fitted below the knee. As I was still in a coma, Michael was concerned that if I continued to move my leg, the weight of the device could cause me to fall out of bed. Alarmed, he raised his concerns with the nurse who was nearby, and she replied, "Don't worry. It's the patients who don't move who may be more of a concern.

Shortly after I was first admitted to A&E, I had been sedated and fitted to a ventilator. Over the next few days the prescribed level of sedation was gradually reduced and eventually stopped. Four days passed, and I continued to be slow to waken. The doctors' concerns about potential brain damage grew, and another CT scan was taken on Tuesday, July 1. The results confirmed their suspicions: I had sustained extensive brain damage. Two blood clots were found, in addition to widespread axonal injury. Axonal injury is a major cause of unconsciousness and persistent coma after head trauma, not a favorable prognosis. When Frances was advised of this development, the doctor told her, "We really don't know how he will be when he wakes up."

The extubation, or removal of the ventilator tube, was attempted a couple of days later, but this proved unsuccessful, and my score on the Glasgow Coma Scale (GCS) dropped to 3. As a result, I was further sedated and reintubated. The GCS is a neurological scale used worldwide to record a patient's level of consciousness after an acute brain injury. The scale ranges from 15 (normal) to 3 (lowest possible score; normally deep coma or death).

But I was spared from death again. Following the earlier failed attempts, the doctors kept trying and I was successfully taken off the ventilator on Thursday, July 3. I was finally capable of steadily breathing on my own. I came out of the coma and even started to say a few words, but I was extremely confused at this stage, and very often what I said didn't make any sense. It's sometimes funny now looking back as my family and I often joke about the details. One afternoon in particular I had started to say, "The main thing. The main thing is!" They all waited in anticipation, expecting a profound or memorable statement such as, "I'm alive! We're all here!" or something similar. But, no. "The main thing is risotto!" I exclaimed. Surprisingly, food must have been on my mind, which I expect was probably a good thing. Nevertheless, real life can be somewhat different from what's portrayed by Hollywood and the movies. We were joking about this one day with friends after recounting the story, and one of them said, "*Risotto* could be a good title for your book!"

My condition was recorded as stable for the first time on Monday, July 7, twelve days after I had been admitted. I was subsequently discharged from intensive care and admitted to the orthopedic trauma unit. I had remained in a coma for most of the twelve days that I been in intensive care. I was admitted to the same orthopedic ward on exactly the same day of the year as my mother had been the previous year. This must have added greatly to the strain my family was experiencing, particularly for my dad and sister. They must have relived some difficult memories of my mother's sad death. I have no doubts that there must have been times when they thought, *Here we go again.*

Frances and me

The medical team at ARI was always very supportive of my family and kept them informed of my progress at all times. I was still confused, to the extent that I had absolutely no idea where I was or the reason I was even there. A doctor tried to explain one day the reasons for this, and how best they could help. He described how what was said to me during this time would be very important, as my brain would be trying to find new pathways to eventually reach the same end result. The example he gave was that "One might be driving from A to B, only to discover the road ahead closed, and the driver would need to find an alternative route around the problem in order to reach the same destination." My family was advised to be very clear in what they said and to try as much as possible not to contradict me but to always be truthful and try not to upset me. However, as I remained confused and what I said was very often muddled, this was to prove more difficult and challenging than expected. As mentioned previously, we sometimes joke about the details now, but on one particular day I had asked my son John if "the flowers were ordered for the festival." Very bemused, he replied, "Yes, that's all taken care of," hoping this would be sufficient to reassure me. I then replied, "Very good. How much did you order?" This level of confusion continued for a number of days, and I continued to spend much of each day asleep. I underwent further surgery on Wednesday, July 9, when my left knee and right ankle were both reconstructed and a combination of titanium plates, wires, and screws were fitted. My body was now held together by a total of sixty-five pieces of titanium.

Most days while I was a patient in the orthopedic trauma unit, Frances helped with feeding during mealtimes, and she was therefore permitted access to the ward before official visiting hours started. Although I don't remember any of this, it was a great help to me. The injury to my brain had been so extensive that I had completely forgotten how to carry out very simple, everyday tasks. For example, Frances remembers one day when there was soup for lunch, and she found me attempting to eat it with a fork. The orthopedic trauma department is always very busy and frequently full to capacity, and although they would have been more than happy to do so if possible, the nurses just didn't have the time required to help feed every patient individually.

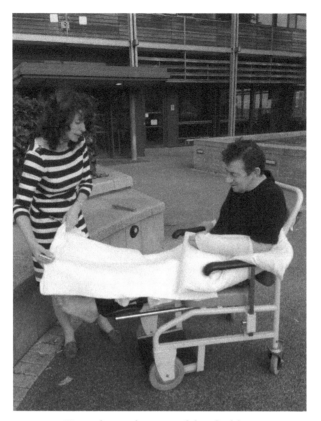

Hospital grounds, in one of the wheelchairs

I was hoisted into a wheelchair for the first time on Sunday, July 13. The weather was excellent that summer, and from then on, Frances took me off the ward almost every afternoon in one of the hospital wheelchairs. Two nurses would transfer me by mechanical hoist into the wheelchair, and Frances and my family would take me out into the fresh air for half an hour or so. The only difficulty with this was that I needed an adapted wheelchair that allowed me to keep both of my legs fully elevated, and there were few of these available. Frances prayed every day for one of these chairs, and every day she found one— sometimes at the door as she came in, sometimes beside the ward, or sometimes elsewhere in the hospital.

With my family in ARI

While these daily events were unfolding in ARI, many friends in Peterhead were a great support to my family. They provided much-needed practical help, including delivering prepared meals and groceries to our home. In the same way, another group of ladies from the church set up a system for the provision of meals as and when required. Our neighbor cut our grass at home for the whole summer. These were all tremendous acts of Christian kindness and love, clearly demonstrating real practical help; the support shown by them all was very much appreciated.

During my time in intensive care and the orthopedic unit, my family traveled to ARI every day, a round trip of approximately sixty miles, or one hour each way. My son-in-law Michael was employed as a surveyor for a certification company based in Aberdeen and was available to drive Frances and the family to intensive care before carrying on to work. This was a tremendous help for Frances, who was constantly tired and felt as if she just didn't have the energy to drive. In addition to being driven there, Frances appreciated the opportunity on the journey home to phone and text the many concerned friends and family who were always anxious to be updated as to my condition.

When I was transferred to orthopedics, either Monica or Frances's mother, June, stepped in and drove her to hospital on alternate days. My sister Grace was a great support, taking my dad through every day and providing sandwiches and so on for the visitors. Michael's employers fully understood the situation and were very accommodating, allowing him to work the flexible hours required to support the family at this time. The company that I worked for in Aberdeen also couldn't have been more supportive. They offered whatever assistance they could and continued to do so throughout, visiting frequently when I was in hospital and later at home. This was far beyond what was required or expected of them. At this early stage, Frances didn't feel able to discuss any details of my condition with them, but again Monica was there to help, and she constantly updated them on my progress.

We received many cards and messages each day, providing much appreciated support and encouragement; they always came at just the right time, when they were most needed. A card received early on from a friend at church contained the following verse from Lamentations.

> … for his compassions never fail. They are new every morning; great is your faithfulness. (3:22–23 NIV)

She had also written a very appropriate message: "Don't overload your boat with worry about tomorrow. He provides fresh manna every day." Very comforting words.

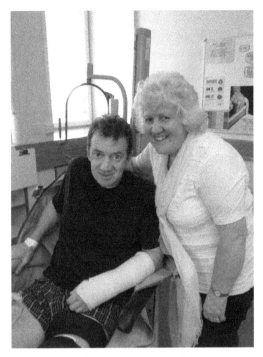

With my sister Grace in ARI

I have very vague recollections of my final days at ARI, and the following memory may well have been when I was taken to the fracture clinic to have staples removed from my legs shortly before I was discharged. A consultant appeared at my bedside and introduced himself, saying he'd been involved with my surgery, and he went on to discuss what had been done to my right ankle. He then asked how my patience was and added, "You will learn from it, as this will be a long, slow healing process." He said that he would probably see me again in about five weeks. I had no idea of the extent of my injuries at the time, but I do remember thinking, *Five weeks doesn't seem too bad.*

My family was praying earnestly that when it was time for me to be discharged from ARI, I would be sent to the right place for rehabilitation. This was proposed to be either Woodend Hospital in Aberdeen or the Ugie (pronounced *yoo-gie*) Hospital in Peterhead. Woodend had a department that specialized in traumatic brain injuries, whereas the Ugie Hospital catered to more general rehabilitation but had the added advantage of being located in Peterhead, which was especially important for my family and the many friends who wanted to visit. It was decided that the most favorable option was for me to be transferred to the Ugie Hospital in Peterhead.

Frances soon realized how important a suitable wheelchair would be for me in Peterhead and prayed many times that one would become available. She contacted a company in Aberdeen that supplied this type of equipment and was told that wheelchairs adapted for keeping the occupant's legs straight and elevated were not easy to come by. The person who would normally deal with this request had just gone on two weeks' annual leave, which meant they would take several weeks to source one. This was disappointing news, but that door was now closed. Three days before my transfer was scheduled to take place, Frances and her sister Monica were sitting on a bench outside the hospital having lunch when a nurse who knew Monica from school came over to inquire about how I was. Frances gave her an update on my progress and the great news that I was due to be transferred to Peterhead for rehabilitation. The difficulty in finding a suitable wheelchair was also mentioned, and the nurse suggested that Frances phone the Ugie Hospital as soon as possible, given that they could take weeks to find one. The following morning Frances phoned and spoke to the occupational therapist, who fully understood the request and promised to do his best but confirmed that they were difficult to source and may take a few weeks. Within half an hour he phoned back and said, "You won't believe this, but we have one here at the hospital"—more answered prayer! The wheelchair was in the Ugie Hospital before I was.

The patient transfer service was booked for Wednesday, July 23, and as I had to make the journey on a stretcher, everything was in place for my move. Unfortunately, my trip was canceled due to sickness in the ward and rescheduled for the following day. Again, I was prevented from traveling that day, and the transfer was again rebooked for the next day. This was now Friday, and a delay with blood test results meant I couldn't go then either. What now? This was the weekend, and the patient transfer service only operated during the week. The only option now was for an emergency ambulance to become available. One would need to arrive at ARI from Peterhead with a patient, and in the off chance there were no more calls and the ambulance was empty on their return trip to Peterhead, it could take me to the Ugie Hospital. We waited all day Saturday and nothing came, then on Sunday morning Frances was reading her Bible and praying that I would be taken to the Ugie at the right time, in God's time that is, and that an ambulance would come. She read this verse:

> Though it linger, wait for it; it will certainly come and
> will not delay.
> (Habakkuk 2:3 NIV)

This was the first Sunday morning since the accident that Frances and Shannon felt able to go to church. An ambulance came to pick me up at three o'clock on Sunday afternoon, and eventually I was on my way to Peterhead. A paramedic sat beside me for the hour-long journey; as muddled as I was, I'm sure I must have tested his patience with my ramblings!

> Sovereign ruler of the skies,
> Ever gracious ever wise,
> All my times are in your hand,
> All events at your command.
> —John Ryland

Our times are in God's hands; our souls are in his keeping.

chapter 6

Rehabilitation

A heart at peace gives life to the body, but envy rots the bones.
—Proverbs 14:30 (NIV)

But he said to me, "My grace is sufficient for you, for my power is made perfect in weakness." Therefore I will boast all the more gladly about my weaknesses, so that Christs power may rest on me. That is why, for Christ's sake, I delight in my weaknesses, in insults, in hardships, in persecutions, in difficulties. For when I am weak, then I am strong.
—2 Corinthians 12:9–10 (NIV)

AFTER MY DISCHARGE from ARI I began my extended period of rehabilitation in the Ugie Hospital in Peterhead. The few memories I have from ARI are vague, but I do remember quite clearly when a nurse first mentioned my transfer to Peterhead. Although this sounds as if it would have been welcome news, I remember being somewhat alarmed and thinking, *Oh, no, this can't be good. Why are they sending me there?* While "the Ugie" is an excellent small hospital in Peterhead, as far as I knew at the time, it was used exclusively as a dementia unit, or for patients suffering from a terminal illness. I sadly thought the only way anyone left there was in a wooden box. The nurse must have seen my reaction and sensed my disappointment, as she quickly reassured me the main function of the hospital was now rehabilitation. I still remember the relief I felt!

Admission to the Ugie Hospital on a Sunday was unusual, and I'm sure it caused the nurses some difficulty and extra work, particularly as staff levels were reduced at the weekend. Nevertheless I settled in to my new surroundings well, and I'm sure it must have felt good to be back at home in Peterhead.

Other than for short periods in a wheelchair, I was mostly confined to a hospital bed for the first few weeks in rehab. As soon as I became strong enough, I was transferred by mechanical hoist every morning to a wheelchair. I'm fairly sure that at this time I had no real understanding of the number of injuries I had suffered or how close to death I had actually come. It must have been several weeks later that I started to appreciate more clearly the true extent of my injuries. This may sound strange given that there were so many surgical scars on my body, my left arm was in a plaster cast, and there was a boot on my right leg and a brace fitted to my left. But I was experiencing no pain or discomfort and had no recollection whatsoever of the events of that day, and I think the reality of it all just didn't sink in. This may well have been due to the effects of a brain injury, which I was totally unaware I was suffering from at the time. As the weeks and months passed, I gradually recovered from some of the mental difficulties I was experiencing, with the result that my thoughts became clearer and less muddled. This was when I first fully realized how very fortunate I was to be alive. As mentioned earlier, I had absolutely no memory of what happened the day of the accident; every detail I knew had been gleaned from the people around me. Many times I heard, "John it's a miracle you're alive" or "a real answer to prayer," and initially I didn't even appreciate the accuracy of these statements. As some of the details of my injuries became clearer to me, I began to grasp more fully how close to death I had been, and I was all the more thankful to be alive and couldn't help but question why my life had been spared. Throughout this period I experienced a remarkable sense of peace; I'm sure the overwhelming number of prayers that were continually petitioned for me were being answered. This experience is still clear to me, yet I can't find the words to explain it, as it says in the book of Philippians, "The peace of God is beyond all human understanding." I don't remember at any time not completely accepting the circumstances I was in and what God had taken me through. I never once doubted anything or even questioned why it had happened. The only question I ever had was, "Why was my life spared?"

Many people made the time to come and visit me in the hospital, including family members, friends, work colleagues, and of course the wider church family. They were always an encouragement to me even though most days I found it exhausting. To begin with, I struggled to recognize some visitors immediately and needed help from Frances. During the conversations that followed, I slowly remembered some details as the gaps in my memory were being filled in. This was a strange feeling and, again, is difficult to describe, particularly when it was someone that I was sure I knew well but just couldn't remember how or why or even a name. It was almost as if small sections of my memory had been erased. Most days I watched a short video clip of Stephanie and Michael's wedding on my iPad. This played a significant part in my recovery; likewise the many people who came to visit had a similar effect. As I began to recognize faces, I seemed to be able to dig up memories of how and why I knew them. Piece by piece, the gaps were being filled in and parts of my memory were restored. This may sound reasonable and understandable looking back now, especially given the brain injury I sustained. However, at the time, I was completely unaware of any brain damage. I was not in any pain, and there were no obvious physical symptoms to indicate brain injury. I was under the impression that I was communicating fine. But as the weeks and months passed, I did become more aware that my thought processes seemed to be a bit slower. But due to my physical injuries everything was slower, and I very likely assumed this was part of the healing process. This may be a normal symptom of a traumatic brain injury, but as my thoughts were not very clear or sharp, the full extent of my mental limitations was not apparent to me.

My orthopedic injuries continued to heal, and I started to become more independent. I think it was at this time that my mental limitations and the cognitive challenges they brought began to become obvious to me, and I expect these symptoms were even more evident to others at the time. Over time, however, my symptoms have continued to improve, and I now feel that as I am more aware of and have accepted my limitations. I can manage my condition better.

My brain is much slower and the processing of information takes a bit longer; when the volume and complexity of the information I receive increases, it becomes all the more challenging. For example, I find it difficult to concentrate when there is more than one conversation taking place or when I am in a room with many people. Any significant increase in noise levels around me can also be challenging. I have described it as being less able to filter background noise or unimportant information. This was particularly difficult to begin with, but I often felt okay at the time and the symptoms did not materialize until later. Thankfully, I now seem to be more aware when I have reached an "overload" condition and try to quietly remove myself from the situation. This in itself is not always straightforward given that my symptoms are not always immediately visible to others, and I'm not surprised when other people find it difficult to understand. In one of my many medical reports, a consultant clearly states that a traumatic brain injury is sometimes referred to as a hidden disability, and because I am walking and talking, it is not particularly obvious to others that there may be complex difficulties.

I'm convinced that completely accepting the whole situation and the resultant positive and thankful attitude I've been given has been hugely beneficial to my recovery. I can fully appreciate how bitterness or hatred of any kind would have a hugely negative effect on anyone's progress back to health. Without the faith and trust I have in Jesus Christ and the comfort and peace he gives, I can't even begin to imagine how difficult it would have been to come through a similar situation. As the very well-known "Footprints in the Sand" poem reads, "During your times of trial and suffering, when you see only one set of footprints, … It was then that I carried you."

> Even though I walk through the darkest valley, I will
> fear no evil, for you are with me; your rod and your
> staff, they comfort me. (Psalm 23:4 NIV)

Physiotherapy would clearly be a significant part of my rehabilitation and began for the first time two days after my arrival in Peterhead on Tuesday, July 29, 2014. It consisted of very small movements of my toes and fingers and continued twice each week. I was also given similar exercises to continue with on my own on the other days, and I went through these every morning while listening to podcasts of various church services. I was unable to read at the time due to double vision, so podcasts were a great help in passing the time and making the exercises slightly less repetitive and monotonous.

A dear friend from church handed me this verse and poem during a visit one afternoon. Confusion was still very much an issue for me, but the verse meant a great deal and has remained close to my heart ever since. It helped me every morning to focus my thoughts on what was important and on how thankful and fortunate I was to be alive.

> Let the morning bring me word of your unfailing
> love, for I have put my trust in you. Show me the
> way I should go, for to you I lift up my soul. (Psalm
> 143:8 NIV)

The first time I heard a similar version of the poem was a few days earlier on a church service podcast from an anniversary service at Peterhead Baptist Church. It's entitled "The End of the Road Is but a Bend in the Road."

> When we feel we have nothing left to give
> And we are sure that the "song has ended"—
> When our day seems over and the shadows fall
> And the darkness of night has descended,

Where can we go to find the strength
To valiantly keep on trying,
Where can we find the hand that will dry
The tears that the heart is crying—

There's but one place to go and that is to God
And, dropping all pretence and pride,
We can pour out our problem without restraint
And gain strength with Him at our side—

And together we stand at life's crossroads
And view what we think is the end,
But God has a much bigger vision
And he tells us it's only a bend—

For the road goes on and is smoother,
And the "pause in the song" is a "rest,"
And the part that's unsung and unfinished
Is the sweetest and richest and best—

So rest and relax and grow stronger,
Let go and let God share your load,
Your work is not finished or ended,
You've just come to "a bend in the road."

(Used with permission of Helen Steiner Rice Foundation Fund, LLC)

I'm sure you'll understand why I found these words an amazing source of encouragement. Peterhead Baptist Church's anniversary weekend is held every September, and the guest speaker that year was Wayne Sutton from Carrubbers Christian Centre in Edinburgh, who spoke for three services. I listened to them several times on podcast; they were entitled "When God Leads by Another Route," "When God Leads to a Dead End," and "When God Leads Us through Dry Places." These messages were very appropriate to my situation, and I was blessed and strengthened by listening to them. They greatly helped me pass a few hours in contemplation of my experience.

John Jr. and me on the promenade by the Ugie Hospital—great to be outside

God blessed us with the driest September on record for Peterhead, and Frances took me outside in the wheelchair most afternoons. We typically took a route along a nearby seafront promenade, which runs alongside the mouth of the River Ugie located just behind the hospital, and being outside in the fresh air with peace and quiet came to be the highlight of every day. The hospital was always comfortable and the nursing staff very kind and helpful, but it just felt great to be outdoors as by this time I had been in the hospital for several months. The term *cabin fever* springs to mind, and this may well have been the case! These calm and peaceful walks contributed greatly to my recovery from the brain injury. We often met people who were out for a leisurely walk along the promenade, and most of them knew about the accident and remembered how serious it was. They sometimes inquired about my injuries and recovery, many times saying how fortunate they thought I was to be alive. Frances and I have unexpectedly met many of these people since then, and they are further amazed having seen my progress. On one occasion during the summer of 2016, Frances and I were in a café when a woman who failed to recognize me told Frances that she had commented to her husband only the day before, "I wonder how that man is doing, the one we used to see in the wheelchair on the prom." She was amazed when she realized that I was there sitting in the café, with no wheelchair and only a walking stick.

Early one afternoon in November, as Frances and I were about to head out on one of these walks, we unexpectedly met my general practitioner in the hospital corridor. I had been a patient of Dr. Donaldson's for almost thirty years, and she was delighted to see me. I'll never forget her words when we met that day: "John, it really is great to see you! I've seen all your notes and records. It really is a miracle you're alive." This was a remarkable comment for a doctor to make, and I found it very humbling.

On September 22, 2014, Frances and I celebrated our silver wedding anniversary; the weather was good, and the hospital was happy for me to go to Stephanie's house for a meal. Frances, Shannon, and John pushed me there in the wheelchair, probably a distance of around one and a half miles. This was definitely a challenge for them as the push was mostly uphill, but it was a great day for me, a very normal experience for a change. It was the first time I had been in their new home and also the first time all six of us had been together for a meal since the accident. This felt great, and I really appreciated the few hours' break from the hospital environment.

Frances and me with Stephanie in her house

I was advised to see an optician in Peterhead regarding my vision difficulties to determine whether glasses might help in the short term. An appointment was arranged for November, and Frances took me there in the wheelchair for various tests and examinations. The results confirmed that reading glasses would help, and I was supplied with a pair as a temporary measure because the prescription was expected to change as the nerve damage healed. Following the appointment, Frances and I went to a local café for coffee, another normal experience that I never would have expected to appreciate so much. The café is owned by lovely Christian friends, who always were a huge encouragement.

David Stephen, an acquaintance from a local church in Peterhead, visited the hospital every Friday. He played the piano and led some informal hymn singing for patients in the dayroom. David provided a great service, and almost every day he would visit a hospital or care home in the area. This was uplifting and an occasion I looked forward to every week, as many of the patients came along and thoroughly enjoyed the opportunity to sing some songs. Even some who had no connection with a church remembered some of the hymns from their childhood and enjoyed the fellowship.

Rev. Jim Clarke, another special friend, also came to visit frequently and always prayed with me. Jim is originally from Ireland but has been in Scotland for many years. On one of his visits, he arrived at the same time as my dad and my sister Grace along with two other visitors. The conversation quickly progressed into full-on "Doric," the local northeast dialect. Shortly afterward, Jim said, "I don't understand a word you're all saying," and we all had a good laugh before reverting to the more proper Queen's English. Jim is a retired pastor and at the time was acting as moderator at Peterhead Baptist Church during a time of pulpit vacancy. He was such an encouragement to me and my family when he came to visit; it always proved to be a positive experience and something I eagerly anticipated. Jim lost his lovely wife, Margaret, to cancer in 2017, and she is very sadly missed. I was very thankful that I was well enough to attend her funeral service.

A local businessman in Peterhead remarked to Frances that on the day of my accident, he could almost tangibly feel the prayer around the town, and he wasn't the only person who made this comment. Frances has said on more than one occasion how much of a comfort it was that the accident took place on a Wednesday, given that most churches in the town had a midweek prayer meeting that night. Prayers were said in numerous churches, meetings in houses, on fishing boats in the North Sea, and many parts of Scotland, and even as far as Hungary and throughout several regions of the United States. It is amazing in itself how quickly prayer requests are passed around through God's people.

chapter 7

Fracture Clinic and Various Outpatient Appointments

Great are the works of the Lord;
they are pondered by all who delight in them.
Glorious and majestic are his deeds, and his righteousness endures forever.
—Psalm 111:2, 3 (NIV)

The hand of the Lord was upon me, and he brought me out by the Spirit
of the Lord and set me in the middle of a valley; it was full of bones.
—Ezekiel 37:1 (NIV)

THROUGHOUT MY RECOVERY it was necessary to attend numerous outpatient appointments at ARI, which took place in a variety of specialist clinics. For the first few months while I was in the Ugie Hospital, I was unable to put any weight on either of my legs and could only be transferred by means of a mechanical hoist, with the result that it was impossible for me to travel by car and the trips to ARI were facilitated by the patient transfer service. This is an excellent service in which patients without transport or those in need of a stretcher or wheelchair are picked up in specialized vehicles and driven to a variety of clinics for appointments. The service is in high demand, so Frances drove herself to each appointment to keep me company once I was there. She was always a great support, and of course another pair of ears was an advantage when it came to understanding and remembering what the doctors and consultants said, as very often the information was just too much for me to retain. Understandably numerous appointments were necessary at the fracture clinic for X-rays, and further appointments were required at general surgery and the eye clinic, all of which were located at ARI. Several appointments also took place at the neuropsychology department and the mobility and rehabilitation service, both of which are located at Woodend Hospital in Aberdeen.

I had frequent scheduled appointments with the fracture clinic, normally every four or five weeks. Given the number of fractures to be checked, X-rays took around an hour and a half to complete on each occasion. The radiologist jokingly remarked at one appointment that Titanium Man had arrived and that they had best advise the other patients that they would have some time to wait! Initially, the fracture clinic requested that I be transferred by stretcher, and this continued even after I was spending most of each day in a wheelchair, as the use of a mechanical hoist around the X-ray table was not possible. I was often reassured by the consultant or registrar that my bones were continuing to heal but weren't yet strong enough to bear any weight. I was repeatedly told that I was making good progress but things would just take more time. I didn't question this and always accepted what the doctors said, but at no time did anyone ever mention whether I would walk again or refer to a future time when I would. I did sometimes wonder why this was the case, as I didn't think fractures took so long to heal. Was there something they were keeping from me? Then one day in October, Frances and I were shown the X-rays for the first time, and I finally understood their lack of optimism.

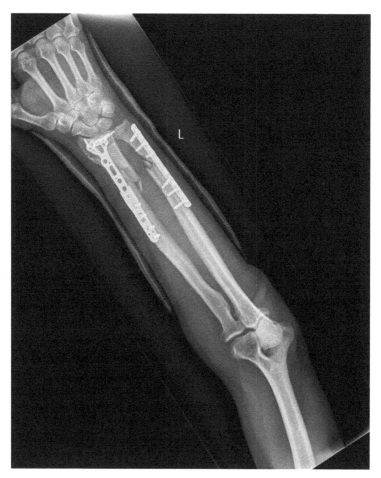

Left forearm

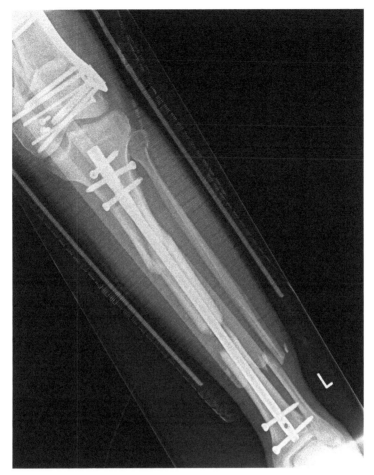

Left femur, knee, tibia, and fibula (note areas of missing bone)

The real extent of the damage to my arms and legs became very clear that day; we were both truly shocked. I remember finding the information difficult to absorb—the sheer number of screws, plates, wires, and nails that had been fitted was remarkable. The registrar asked how my spine was at the same appointment. I didn't even remember that there were two fractures in my spine. She then added something I'll never forget: "The two bones in your upper arms are the only long bones in your body that weren't fractured."

As we viewed the X-rays, the registrar identified several areas in both of my legs and my left forearm where there were whole sections of bone missing. Seeing this immediately explained why the fractures were taking so long to heal and why I had been mostly confined to a hospital bed.

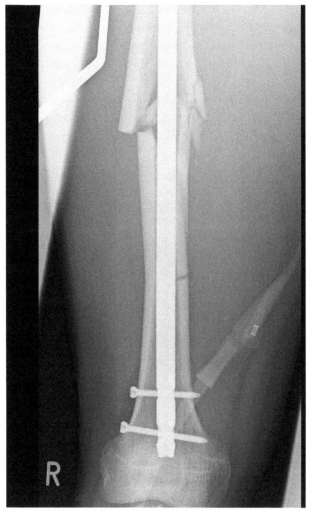

Right femur

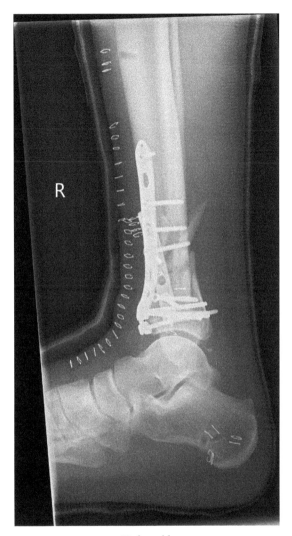

Right ankle

More patience would be required until sufficient bone had grown. I fully understood and accepted this as the X-ray images confirmed that any weight bearing at this time would simply be impossible. Transfers from the hospital bed to and from a wheelchair would continue by means of mechanical hoist. When I was stronger, I was hoisted into a wheelchair to sit for longer periods and began to eat my meals along with the other patients in the communal dining area. I was allocated a single room for most of the time I spent in the Ugie Hospital, and this privacy suited me. Nevertheless, the interaction with other patients during mealtimes was beneficial to me and very much encouraged by the nursing staff.

A positive outcome taken from the X-rays was that my right forearm had now completely healed. This was great news, and an appointment was made with the Mobility and Rehabilitation Service (MARS) for me to be measured for a single-arm-operated wheelchair. This took place a few weeks later, and I remember joking with the nurses while I was waiting on the transfer vehicle that I would see them later, as I was off to MARS for the day. At the clinic I was measured and surprised to be informed that they had a perfectly fitting wheelchair in stock and available for me to use. This was completely unexpected as we had been advised it would take several weeks for a suitably sized chair to be built, and I believe this was another answer to prayer. In addition, before I left the center with the new wheelchair, they checked the serial number on the old one and said they would keep it as it belonged to them and should never have been in the Ugie Hospital in the first place. This further confirmed the original answered prayer for a suitable wheelchair to be in place.

This new wheelchair took some time to get used to, but it was a much-needed source of independence. I was now hoisted into the wheelchair every morning and could move around the room or along the corridor at any time on my own. I could meet Frances at the door of the hospital during visiting time and also make my way by myself to the dining area for meals. Over time and with practice, as I grew stronger, I was able to transfer myself to and from the wheelchair by means of sliding along a banana board (wooden, banana-shaped plywood board), which was great and meant no more need for the mechanical hoist. The ability to move around the room and visit the toilet, for example, on my own gave me an even greater sense of independence. I remember the first time I went to the sink in the bathroom to wash my hands and face; this was a big step, as before this, I had been restricted to a bed bath and the use of disposable wipes. As I attempted to wring out the facecloth, I was forced to give up as I didn't have nearly enough strength. This was when I first fully realized how physically weak I was, as this seemed like such a normal activity that I could have done before without thought or effort.

I also attended an outpatient appointment at general surgery during October 2014. The consultant was very pleased to see me and advised that he had been the physician on duty at A&E when I was first admitted. Following an examination of my abdomen, he explained how he and his team had helped stop the bleeding and were able to save my spleen by gluing the tear. But on the whole, he felt his contribution was fairly minimal in comparison with the treatment demanded by my other injuries. I was sitting in a wheelchair at the appointment, and he remarked more than once how amazed he was to see me move my legs. He remembered very clearly viewing my initial scans and X-rays and said the damage was extensive.

I returned again to the fracture clinic on November 26, 2014, for more X-rays and more good news. Sufficient bone growth had now occurred to allow me to attempt to weight bear on my right leg; this was long-awaited and welcome news. The doctor also said my left arm was now strong enough to use for smaller tasks. I would need to continue wearing the brace, but it could now be removed for washing. The following day, the physiotherapist in Peterhead contacted the fracture clinic to confirm exactly how much weight I should put on my right leg. Subsequently, under the guidance of the therapists and with the help of a "pulpit frame," I stood up for a few seconds on Friday, November 28, 2014. This was a real landmark in my recovery, being the first time I had stood in over five months. It was an amazing feeling, albeit with all my weight only on one leg.

There remained a substantial area of missing bone in my left tibia, and although the titanium rod in place provided some additional strength, it was only enough for partial weight bearing. Over the next few days and with more practice, I progressed to using a walking frame, which eventually became the means by which I transferred to and from a wheelchair. This gradual progress continued, and people often said, "You're doing well, as long as you're making small steps of progress," an unintentionally humorous choice of words, I suspect, as they really were small steps!

We continued with the physiotherapy, and the next significant milestone was on Friday, December 5, when I managed to climb four steps with the help of a handrail and an elbow crutch. Although significant damage had occurred to both legs, my left knee in particular had been completely smashed and remained very weak. Two physiotherapists were present, and I will never forget the instructions they gave me that day: "John, it's easy to remember the procedure for stairs—good leg first when going up, and bad leg first when going down. Good up to heaven, and bad down to Hades."

My first appointment at Horizons Rehabilitation Centre in Aberdeen was also in October. I met with a neuropsychologist who commented on my remarkable recovery. She said, "Considering the brain injury you sustained it really is quite amazing that we are sitting here having this conversation." Several tests were undertaken, and then a full neuropsychological assessment was recommended. This would have to wait until I was discharged from the hospital, as a more normal environment at home was considered to provide more accurate results. The assessment went ahead in February 2016 and consisted of various cognitive tests. I was given a range of tasks to complete that measured immediate memory, visuospatial functioning, language, attention, and delayed memory. Results showed a decline in my processing speed and significant evidence of symptoms of fatigue, particularly when I was placed under moderate demand. These cognitive deficits were consistent with the type of brain injury I had sustained, and the doctor remarked, "Given the damage done to your brain was so widespread and extensive, you have made quite a remarkable recovery." A detailed report including future employment recommendations formed a significant part of the assessment, and in her conclusion the neuropsychologist stated, "Given Mr. Buchan's remarkable physical recovery and his relatively intact language ability, I suspect the subtle nature of residual cognitive difficulties he continues to experience may not be obvious to others. This may result in his true abilities being overestimated. One has to bear in mind that the assessment was undertaken in ideal conditions, with limited demands. I think it would be difficult for him to perform in a demanding and rapidly changing environment such as his previous employment." I fully agreed with the doctor's summary, which confirmed the difficulty I have when trying to explain my situation to other people. It was also reassuring to know that someone else completely understood the difficulties I was experiencing and could endorse my own feelings regarding my abilities, as well as empathizing with my condition.

chapter 8

Discharged

In that day you will say:
"Give praise to the Lord, proclaim his name;
make known among the nations what he has done,
and proclaim that his name is exalted."

—Isaiah 12:4 (NIV)

By faith in the name of Jesus, this man whom you see and know was
made strong. It is Jesus name and the faith that comes through him
that has given this complete healing to him, as you can all see.

—Acts 3:16 (NIV)

I WAS DISCHARGED from the Ugie Hospital on Tuesday, December 9, and went home for the first time after a total of 167 days in the hospital. This was fantastic progress, and to be considered medically fit and strong enough to leave was a great feeling. However, it was a massive adjustment for me following such a lengthy period under medical supervision and also brought a degree of apprehension. My occupational therapist and her assistant met Frances and me at our home to ensure I could get in without any mishaps. Our house was located at the top of a hill and there was a considerable slope on the driveway, but fortunately it was possible to drive the car directly into the garage and then access the house by means of about ten steps to the door—still a huge challenge for me. I remember being thoroughly exhausted afterward and was glad the therapists were there to provide support if required. They also brought the additional equipment I would need to use around the home (toilet and shower seats, etc.) to ensure my comfort and safety. It was a great feeling to be back at home in familiar surroundings, but the whole experience was very tiring. I used the wheelchair to get around the house from room to room and a walking frame to help with the few steps required to transfer to a seat or into bed. These things all took some time to get used to, but I soon settled into my new routine.

Christmas Day came soon after, and we spent a wonderful day at Frances's mother and father's house along with the rest of her family. Throughout the entire day I couldn't stop thinking about how very privileged I was that my life had been spared and I had been granted this opportunity to spend another Christmas with my family.

Christmas Day 2014 with some of Frances's family

The following Sunday I attended Peterhead Baptist Church for the first time since the accident. I was surprised and moved to be greeted by applause from the entire congregation as I went into the church. I was in a wheelchair, and no doubt they had just seen a very visible answer to their many prayers. Jim Gordon was the visiting speaker that week, and he publicly prayed for me, exactly one month after I stood up for the first time. To be there was a fantastic feeling and very emotional, but again I found the whole experience mentally exhausting. It felt as if I just couldn't process the added information that came when in the company of several people at once, and this continued for several months but has since gradually improved. During the first few months, particularly following a somewhat busy day, I very often didn't sleep much at night. I would wake up in the early hours of the morning and lie awake while my mind would go over and over the details that were discussed the previous day, as if trying to process the information. Strangely enough, the subjects of the conversations weren't necessarily anything that troubled me. This was understandably very tiring; however, these symptoms have also slowly improved, as I have learned to manage the condition better and I try to avoid the situations that cause these difficulties whenever possible.

At the beginning of the following year (2015) I completed an application for a blue badge (disability badge for the car), even though it took me two days to complete the online application. Fortunately, the badge was granted straight away and arrived just in time for an appointment at the eye clinic at ARI, where parking nearby could be very problematic—more answered prayer. During the second week of January, when I attended the appointment at the eye clinic, the orthoptist conducted a thorough investigation and was confident that the double vision I was experiencing was the result of damage sustained by the nerves that controlled the movement of my eyes, suggesting this may improve as the nerves continued to heal. A few days later, I was back for another appointment, and this time the consultant ophthalmologist also conducted a thorough examination and said, "You really are very lucky, Mr. Buchan. I've seen patients with a far smaller knock to the head who completely lost their sight."

We arrived home from the appointment to find that a book entitled *90 Minutes in Heaven* had been left at our house. Very briefly, it's about a pastor in America who, when driving home from a conference, was involved in a fatal car crash. The emergency medical technicians at the scene conducted a thorough examination and found no pulse or any sign of life, so the man's body was covered with a tarpaulin until the authorities arrived to officially declare him deceased. A passing pastor who had attended the same conference stopped his car as he felt called to pray for what he thought was an injured driver. Even though he was informed by the paramedics that the driver had died, he went to the wreckage and prayed for the man. Ninety minutes later, the man began to breathe. It is a remarkable story. This book, along with the encouragement I've received from many friends, has played a major part in my sharing my story in *Spared by Grace*. The book *90 Minutes in Heaven* opens with the words, "To the prayer warriors, they prayed, I'm here." The first time I read this, I just thought, *This could have been written for me*, as the statement really sums up my life.

Two weeks later I was back at the fracture clinic for more X-rays, and yet again we were given more good news. I was advised to gradually wean myself off the supportive boot on my right ankle, and I could also slowly wean off the splint on my left arm. This was encouraging progress, but the concerns remained regarding my left tibia, as there was still no evidence of any significant bone growth.

Sometime afterward, Frances and I were in a café in Peterhead when we met a nurse who had been at my bedside one day in intensive care; she recognized Frances immediately and was delighted to see us. She really was quite amazed to see me using a walking frame as she said they were sure in intensive care that I would have to lose both my legs.

Joint birthday party in June 2015; Shannon's twenty-first and my forty-ninth—
A happy day, lots of ice cream and cake

My father sadly suffered a stroke one evening during the summer of 2015 and spent several months in various hospitals; he was unable to walk, and numerous care options were considered to determine whether he could return home to his own house. Although he remained mentally sharp, these options were not practical and he was discharged from the hospital with a care plan that initially allowed him to stay with my sister Grace in her home. On the first of March the following year, Grace drove my father and me to Edinburgh to attend his older brother's funeral. This was a sad day, but it was good for the three of us to be able to spend time together. My dad was admitted to the hospital on Wednesday, March 30, 2016, and peacefully passed away two days later, going home to be with his Lord. This again was a very sad time for us as a family. I was close to my father and would say we grew closer as the years went on. He was a very kind, quiet, and generous man who really lived out his faith; I had great respect for him and miss him very much. At his funeral service, James Macmillan, a dear friend and the minister at my dad's church, spoke of my dad's favorite scripture: "I know that my redeemer lives" (Job 19:25 NIV). He also likened his trials over the last few years to those of Job, but like Job, my father's faith never wavered.

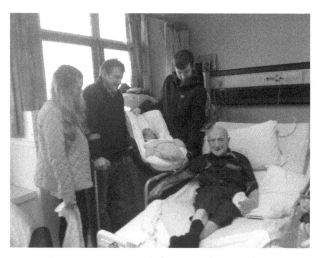

Four generations: my dad, me, Stephanie with her husband Michael, and Michael Jr.

At one of my many neuropsychology appointments, I asked whether I would ever be permitted to drive again. The doctor advised that given the extent of the brain injury I had suffered, I would need to be referred to the Scottish Driving Assessment Service in Edinburgh. She added that if this was something that I felt able to apply for, it might be prudent to make inquiries, as there could be a considerable waiting time in processing applications. I was referred by my general practitioner and undertook the off-road assessment on June 30, 2016, in the SMART Center at the Astley Ainsley Hospital in Edinburgh. My reaction times during a number of different tasks and situations were measured, mostly conducted on a specialized test rig. I performed well in the assessment, but because I suffered from double vision, approval to proceed with the on-road assessment would need to come directly from the driving authorities. Following an investigation by their medical team and consultation with my ophthalmologist, permission was granted and I underwent an on-road assessment on Tuesday, December 13. This also took place in Edinburgh and was far more extensive than I expected. Upon completion, the occupational therapist who conducted the assessment said she would send a report to the Driver and Vehicle Licensing Agency recommending that they reissue my driving license; the only restriction stipulated was that I would be limited to driving a car with an automatic transmission. Gaining permission to drive again was never a big concern of mine, but it was a great relief when it was over and I received the confirmation that I was capable to drive, as this was further progress in the journey to regaining my independence.

chapter 9

Recovery, Further Surgery, and Outpatient Physiotherapy

You need to persevere so that when you have done the will
of God, you will receive what he has promised.
—Hebrews 10:36 (NIV)

Great peace have they who love your law,
and nothing can make them stumble.
—Psalm 119:165 (NIV)

ONE SUNDAY AFTERNOON back when I was a patient in the
Ugie Hospital, I had been at my daughter Stephanie's house for lunch.
The weather was good so again we made the journey in the wheelchair.
We were making our way back to the hospital later in the afternoon
when I suddenly felt a sharp pain in my left knee as we crossed a curb
on the pavement. The pain slowly eased as the afternoon progressed,
but I mentioned it when I got back to the ward. The duty nurse
discovered a small, sharp bump on top of my knee, and a small bandage
was applied to provide some protection to the area. A doctor came to
investigate the following morning and after an examination decided
things should wait until X-rays were taken, as I was due to be seen at

the fracture clinic in a few days' time. The X-rays revealed a broken tension wire on my left kneecap; the consultant remarked that this was not uncommon with the type of injury I had suffered. Given the fact that the wire had served its purpose, it could now be removed. Providing the wire didn't puncture the skin, the surgery wasn't urgent. The discussion returned to my left tibia, where the one-and-a-half-inch section of bone was missing, and various options for repair were discussed. Ultimately it was decided to refer me to another orthopedic consultant who specialized in this type of surgery.

My first appointment with the consultant, Mr. Ashcroft, took place at Woodend Hospital on February 20, 2015. Dr. Neely was also present, and after studying the X-rays in detail, they discussed the various options that were open to me, including bone grafts. It became clear during the conversation that Dr. Neely had been on duty at A&E when I was first admitted on the day of the accident. He commented more than once how amazed he was at my progress. Mr. Ashcroft's words were, "Your recovery is quite amazing, considering your extensive injuries; I wouldn't have been surprised if any one of the fractures had taken three years to recover from, never mind the inevitable complications, but to have them all together and be sitting here like this really is quite amazing." They agreed that I should return to Woodend Hospital in April for surgery, when they would insert a compound (Ignite C) into my left tibia exactly where the section of bone was missing. This was described to me as a man-made compound that would be mixed with my stem cells and injected into the area to encourage bone growth. The broken wire on my knee would also be removed during the same procedure. Just as Frances and I were leaving the appointment, the consultant also said, "Mr. Buchan, it's been great to meet you. Although we've never met before, I know all about you." He then laughed, saying, "Your X-rays were on display in the tea room for weeks."

I had no concerns about the surgery itself, but again the risk of infection was very real. I was admitted to Woodend Hospital for surgery on April 15, 2015. As I lay on my bed waiting to be taken to the operating room, I was reading my Bible and came to the story of

Jesus healing a paralytic man in the book of Mark. When Jesus told the paralyzed man his sins were forgiven, some of the teachers of the law who were there thought he was blaspheming. Jesus then asked the teachers,

> "Why are you thinking these things? Which is easier: to say to the paralytic, 'Your sins are forgiven' or to say, 'Get up, take your mat and walk?' But that you may know that the Son of Man has authority on earth to forgive sins." … '*He said to the paralytic "I tell you, get up, take your mat and go home*." He got up, took his mat and walked out in full view of them all. This amazed everyone and they praised God, saying, "We have never seen anything like this." (Mark 2:8–12 NIV)

The answer to the question Jesus asked of the teachers of the law became very clear to me that day. Even those of us who know Jesus personally and have received his amazing gift of salvation can at times limit his power. Why should we be amazed or even surprised when he answers prayer and performs (for him) a fairly routine miracle? I felt at complete peace and knew within myself that if it was God's will, he would take me through this again. The surgery was far more extensive than expected as the wire had broken in several places, but ultimately, it went very well, and I was discharged the following day. Recovery began again!

On crutches at a favorite country park, great progress

I met with the consultant again six weeks later, and Mr. Ashcroft was very satisfied with my progress. He showed me X-rays that showed some small evidence of bone growth. He advised me to carry on with physiotherapy and said he would see me again in three months. This was good news, and he seemed optimistic with regard to my progress. At the next appointment, he asked various questions about my range of movement, how my physiotherapy was coming along, and whether I was experiencing any pain or discomfort. He then said, "We have discussed your case in detail and have decided not to carry out further X-rays today. We think this will be a slow healing process, and it may be too soon to see any more significant growth. We also think you've traveled to hospital in Aberdeen often enough. We would like you to continue with physiotherapy, and we'll see you again in one year's time."

Mr. Ashcroft also said they were confident that the nails and screws were strong enough, and I should work along with my physiotherapist to reduce my reliance on the elbow crutches.

Physiotherapy continued every week, when one morning probably around May or June, I mentioned to the physiotherapist, Maggie, that my daughter was expecting a baby in November. We joked about my becoming a grandfather, and the physiotherapist then said, "That really is wonderful news. Now you should set yourself a new goal and see who'll be walking unaided first—you or the baby." Internally I assured myself, *Obviously that will be me, as the baby won't be born until November. Does she remember it will take a further year after that before the baby will be able to walk!* Unknown to me at the time, the physiotherapist was expecting her second child at the time and therefore knew exactly what she was saying. My grandson was born in late October that year, and it's amazing how accurate Maggie was in her assessment. One year later during October 2016, both Michael Jr. and I took our first few steps unaided, although it didn't take him long to overtake me.

On another occasion during physiotherapy, I was attending a lower limb class along with three other patients. The class took place weekly and was in addition to my individual appointments; a new staff member had been transferred to the Peterhead department and came into the class to meet us. Each patient was introduced, and a brief summary was given of their injuries and treatment. When they came to me, the physiotherapist told the new staff member, "Here's John, our little miracle! I'll let him explain his injuries himself." I gave a brief description of the injuries to my limbs, and I'll never forget the look on her face. She seemed completely bewildered, as if she questioned whether I was being truthful. She then asked how long I had been attending physio and seemed even more amazed when I told her.

During one of my scheduled appointments at Woodend Hospital, the orthopedic consultant said he thought it was very likely that I would develop significant arthritis at some point in the future, especially considering the damage done to so many of my joints. I mentioned this during physiotherapy a few days later and asked if anything could be done to reduce the likelihood or at least slow the onset. The physiotherapist,

Leslie, replied "Oh, we don't need to believe that. You've already broken the rule book. You shouldn't even be able to walk."

At one of my final appointments I gave a printed copy of my X-rays to the department. They were delighted and said they would be used to help encourage new students. Physiotherapy continued and the appointments slowly reduced in frequency, my last two being at three-month intervals. Following ninety-nine outpatient appointments, I was finally discharged from Peterhead Physiotherapy Department on November 1, 2017. I do, however, continue with exercises most days. They are important and have been described as my building blocks for each day. I also try to go swimming each week, and weather permitting Frances and I walk as often as possible, usually at our favorite country park. This is the new normal for me, and I wouldn't change any of it.

Today—One of many walks, coffee first of course

chapter 10

Wedding Ring: More Answered Prayer

If you believe, you will receive whatever you ask for in prayer.
—Matthew 21:22 (NIV)

They comforted and consoled him over all the trouble the Lord had brought upon him, and each one gave him a piece of silver and a gold ring.
—Job 42:11 (NIV)

AS WAS MENTIONED briefly in chapter 4, one of the doctors gave Frances my wedding ring shortly before I was taken to the operating room on that first day. Frances put the ring on her thumb and kept it on that day and night and throughout the following day. The ring gave her some comfort, and she found it difficult to take off but does remember thinking that it wasn't good for her to wear it all the time. The following morning was Friday, June 27, and when Frances woke up there was no ring on her thumb. At first she was relieved, thinking she had been able to take it off during the night. However, when she began to look, it was nowhere to be found. She searched everywhere—bedside cabinet, drawers, the dressing table, everywhere she thought it could be.

The only other people who knew it was missing were our children and son-in-law, who were all staying in the house at the time. They helped look by taking out all the drawers and moving the bed; they searched through the bed sheets and examined the mattress. Throughout the next few days they looked everywhere; they were convinced Frances had the ring when they got home from hospital that night, but they checked with intensive care anyway and searched the car. As they continued to search, Frances prayed about it many times. One night as she was reading from the book of Job, God spoke to her through his word. In 42:11 (NIV; see above) after all Job's trials, it reads, "and each one gave him a gold ring," and she thought, *I'll get that ring back*. It really seemed impossible, but Frances continued to believe and left it with the Lord in prayer.

Personally I had no idea that the ring was even missing until around eight months after the accident. We had returned home from another routine appointment at the fracture clinic, where the splint on my left arm had been permanently removed. I went to try my wedding ring on but couldn't find it in the usual bedside cabinet and asked Frances where it might be. She then proceeded to tell me the whole story, and she got very upset and broke down in tears. I reassured her that, given the circumstances and what we'd come through, I really felt like there was no need to get so upset. It was only a ring, and we could have it replaced. Frances, however, was very upset and wanted *that* ring back, and she continued to pray.

Three months passed, and Frances found herself in the same jeweler's shop where we had bought the rings many years earlier and asked if a gentleman's ring exactly the same as hers could be sourced. The jeweler checked and told her that this was possible, but in order to ensure a perfect match they would need to send her ring to the manufacturers, which could take several weeks. Frances decided against this, as she didn't want to part with another ring, and also realized that replacing the ring would demonstrate a lack of faith in God's ability to restore the original to us.

Another two months passed when my sister Grace phoned one evening to say she'd received a very unusual message through social media from a young woman who'd found a man's wedding ring engraved "John & Frances 22/9/89." Grace said, "I know it's not John's ring as I saw the doctor give it to you in hospital on the day of the accident, but I thought I had better check." Frances then told her the whole story. Earlier in the year, Frances had bought a new tumble dryer, and when it was delivered to the house the faulty machine was taken away. It had subsequently been repaired and resold. The woman who bought the machine was checking to ensure it was clean, put her hand in underneath the lint filter, and pulled out my wedding ring along with some lint! Frances had checked the tumble dryer many times, but the young woman must have had smaller hands and was able to reach further into the machine. On discovering the ring, she asked her mother if she knew anyone called John and Frances. Amazingly, the woman's mother had gone to school with my sister Grace, but they hadn't spoken in many years as the mother had lived abroad and only recently returned to Peterhead. They had unexpectedly met in the supermarket a few days earlier, and as they caught up with one another, the accident was mentioned and our names had been fresh in her mind. We arranged to meet the girl the following morning on our way to church, and she gave us the ring back.

This was yet another clear example of answered prayer. God doesn't only care about the big challenges we face. While many prayers were visibly answered and my life was spared, he equally cares about our day-to-day worries—nothing is too small to bring before him. God really is truly amazing!

Cast all your anxiety on him for he cares for you. (1 Peter 5:7 NIV)

chapter 11

Baptism and Testimony

Consider it pure joy, my brothers and sisters, whenever
you face trials of many kinds, because you know that
the testing of your faith produces perseverance.
—James 1:2, 3 (NIV)

Repent and be baptised, every one of you, in the name of Jesus Christ for
the forgiveness of your sins. And you will receive the gift of the Holy Spirit.
—Acts 2:38 (NIV)

BY AROUND MID-MARCH 2016, baptism had been on my mind
for a few months, but I questioned my physical ability. When I felt I
was strong enough, I mentioned it to Frances during a walk one day.
She was delighted and told me she had been praying for this for over
twenty years. I then spoke with my dear friend Thomas Stephen,
who serves as a deacon at our local church, and David McCaig, the
pastor at Peterhead Baptist Church, and the service was arranged for
Sunday, May 8, 2016. The first time I discussed this with Tom was on
a Wednesday evening, and later that same night my father was taken ill
and admitted to the hospital. Sadly, he never recovered and was taken
home to be with the Lord two days later on Friday, April 1, 2016, and

I never got the opportunity to tell him. He would have been so happy and proud.

I met with the pastor to discuss the details along with another woman from church who had also asked to be baptized. We both gave him a brief summary of how we had come to faith and what had brought us to this point. I remember saying to David that at a service when he was a visiting speaker, I left the church feeling like I had been personally asked, "Is what God has done in your life not reason enough to be baptized?" This question in effect sealed the decision for me; I was clearly prompted by the Holy Spirit to take this step of faith.

David requested that we both share our testimonies at the baptismal service and said that he would also like copies printed so they could be included with the church notices. I had never seen or heard of this being done before and wasn't sure I was entirely comfortable with the idea of writing my story for other people to read. However, David insisted; even if we felt unable to read out the details on the night, he would like them printed because a personal story is a very powerful thing. The service went smoothly, and I found sharing my testimony was the most challenging part. I had prayed about this many times and was satisfied and felt at peace with what I had prepared. I didn't feel nervous when I went forward to speak either, but I did get emotional. Sharing the details of the many things God had taken my family and I through to a packed church seemed to make everything very real. This is remarkable, really; to prepare and print my testimony for people to read was just not something I would have considered, never mind for them to be handed out. The service was broadcast on YouTube via the church website and has been viewed many times; it really is an amazing and visible account of what God has done in my life. Shannon, my youngest daughter, jokingly said that I should have slipped while going into the tank, and the service would have gone viral!

This following is my testimony as I read it that night:

You are the God who performs miracles. (Psalm 77:14 NIV)

Before I go any further I would like to thank you for your prayers. There is absolutely no doubt in my mind the only reason I'm here is because those prayers were answered.

I had a great childhood and was privileged to be brought up in a Christian home and attended Sunday school as a youngster. I never doubted the existence of God, but other than that I don't remember giving it much thought.

I left school at sixteen and went fishing, and slipped into some things during my late teenage years which I'm not proud of. I met Frances when I was about twenty and started coming along here, initially to please Frances, I expect, but that's young love for you. However I soon began to enjoy coming to church.

I can't give you the exact date I was saved but clearly remember the message about the wide and narrow roads and no matter what we thought, we were either on one or the other. Clearly this was for me, as I saw myself on the fence. I asked the Lord for his forgiveness and to come into my heart that night, and it was the best decision I ever made.

The following years were busy with life. We got married, I became skipper, we had three great children, then we got a second boat, etc. We often worked away from home so I was frequently at sea over the weekend, but I still enjoyed coming to church and hearing God's word when I was at home, but again looking back I'm not sure I ever really put my faith first....

The business was sold in 2003; I worked on research vessels for a few years, and then got a job ashore in Aberdeen in 2011....

Now to 2014, as some of you know, this was when the biggest change in my life took place.

I have no memory of the accident or the three to four weeks afterward, so some of the following details are gleaned from Frances, family members, police, and NHS staff.

At 06:45 on Wednesday 25th June 2014, I left for work and was involved in a car crash a few miles from my house. I was cut out the car and airlifted to Aberdeen Royal Infirmary. The other driver sadly died....

Shortly afterward the police arrived at my house and advised Frances I'd been seriously injured in a road accident. Frances and the family then made their way to ARI; a doctor at A&E listed the injuries and stated quite clearly how serious they were. His words were, "Normally, we wouldn't expect someone with these injuries to make it to hospital." Extensive surgery followed—thirteen hours the first day, followed by two further eight-hour operations. The injuries were two collapsed lungs, skull fracture, brain injury, lacerated spleen, two lumbar spine fractures, and extensive fractures to both legs and forearms. A doctor said one day in the fracture clinic, "Your upper arms are the only long bones in your body that weren't fractured."

The result now is a total of sixty-five pieces of metal holding my body together.

To survive the accident really was nothing short of a miracle....

I spent twelve days in intensive care, eleven of which I was in a coma. Frances and I have often discussed this. She describes intensive care as a "real leveler." It doesn't matter who you are, what you have, or what you've done. Everyone is in the same position; suddenly life is so precious, and the only thing that really matters is if you have Jesus Christ as your Savior or if you don't. Without Christ there is no hope; there's nothing! With Christ there is great hope no matter what happens.

> For what hope has the godless when he is cut off, when God takes away his life? (Job 27:8 NIV)

> For death is the destiny of every man; the living should take this to heart. (Ecclesiastes 7:2 NIV)

The whole experience has made this very real to me. I realize death is something we are all aware of but don't often think about. I'm sure it hadn't crossed my mind as I left for work that morning.… I would urge you all to give serious thought to where you'll spend eternity. It's a free choice. Death can come with no warning at any time! We have no control of this.

One night in intensive care a consultant advised Frances I had an infection from the ventilator. He went on to say, "Fingers crossed, because if the infection spreads to the metalwork, we can't treat it." Now we won't go into the pointless "Fingers crossed" statement, but Frances texted family and close friends and asked them to specifically pray against infection. … Remarkably the infection never spread and completely cleared up; despite the extensive compound fractures I never took another infection throughout my six months in hospital. On one particular occasion the entire orthopedic ward had a stomach bug; every patient was affected, including some staff, but again this was kept from me. Remember the lacerated spleen; according to the NHS one of the main functions of the spleen is to help fight infection.

> The prayer of a righteous man is powerful and effective. (James 5:16 NIV)

A doctor said one day, "John, it's a miracle you're alive," but there have been several doctors, consultants, and medical staff who have expressed their amazement at my recovery. Again, more answered prayer.

I am living proof of what prayer can do. I've been at times quite overwhelmed by the number of people who have prayed for me, many times people I'd never met before. It's quite amazing how prayer requests are passed throughout God's people.

> If you believe, you will receive whatever you ask for in
> prayer. (Matthew 21:22 NIV)

Another surprising unexplained fact—throughout the whole experience I've felt no pain.

People have made many comments on the accident and injuries, such as, "That's amazing," "You're very lucky," or sometimes, "Oh, it's a good thing you were in a BMW" or "Oh, you're so lucky there was an off-duty nurse and paramedic immediately on the scene." All these things may have helped; however, the police were surprised I hadn't died immediately from internal injuries. I am living proof that God is in control of all things, and if it's his will, he still continues to perform miracles.

> He performs wonders that cannot be fathomed,
> miracles that cannot be counted. (Job 5:9 NIV)

It's also been said, "You're doing so well; you're so patient." However, Philippians 4:6–7 (NIV) explains this better than I could. It says,

> Do not be anxious about anything, but in everything,
> by prayer and petition, with thanksgiving, present
> your requests to God. And the peace of God, which
> transcends all understanding, will guard your hearts
> and minds in Christ Jesus.

I can't explain the peace and comfort I've been given throughout this whole experience. Undoubtedly, I've been held up by prayer, but it really is beyond all understanding. I don't remember at any time not accepting the situation God had put me in. I never once doubted or questioned it. I really was so thankful to be alive. The only question I've ever had, and still do, was, *Why was I spared?*

The whole thing has indeed been life changing, but more importantly for me it's been faith changing. I feel so much closer to God, and I've been given a completely different perspective on life. It's sad that it took a near-death experience for me to see this.

To summarize, here are two verses from Hebrews 12 (NIV): verse 7 reads, "Endure hardship as discipline," and verses 11–13 read,

> No discipline seems pleasant at the time, but painful. Later on, however, it produces a harvest of righteousness and peace for those who have been trained by it. Therefore, strengthen your feeble arms and weak knees! "Make level paths for your feet," so that the lame may not be disabled, but rather healed.

David asked the question at a service here last year, "Is what God has done in your life not reason enough to be baptized?" Well, that's the reason I'm here tonight.

A favorite verse of Frances's to finish:

> For the man who was miraculously healed was over forty years old. (Acts 4:22 NIV)

chapter 12

My Story: Distribution

To you O Lord I called, to the Lord I cried for mercy;
"What gain is there in my destruction, in my going down into the pit?
Will the dust praise you?
Will it proclaim your faithfulness?
Hear, O Lord, and be merciful to me; O Lord, be my help."
—Psalm 30:8–10 (NIV)

THROUGHOUT THE WEEKS that followed my baptism service, Frances and I distributed the remaining few copies of my story that were left over. Many people commented on how amazing it was that I had survived and sometimes asked for additional copies, so we started to print some more. Since that time, we have made a few small changes to the text and added a photograph of the car to the front page. We have handed out several thousand copies of "my story," and we are still encouraged by the reaction we get from people. This is particularly obvious when they see the photograph of the car on the front. Some local people remembered the accident and how serious it was, and they are frequently amazed when they see my recovery. Many questions regarding the horrific injuries and recovery inevitably follow, so a printed story with details of the miraculous things God has taken my family and me through has been a great way of sharing the whole at the Waterfront Hall on Thursday evening and meet your lovely wife Frances whose wonderful smile told me everything and why you are still standing. You had EVERYTHING to live for, and deep down your subconscious knew that. A lovely wife, three great children, a faith that was strong and empowering, and a community of friends (church and wider family) who believed you could be healed. As the quote says … 'the directions are always within'. The Holy Spirit was at work in your life John and you are a living testimony of that.

We are all here for a purpose and your purpose now is to meet with people and let them know in your own quiet and modest way that you were 'saved' for a purpose. Your remarkable story will cause people to think and ask questions about the meaning of life. Our savior lives. Ephesians 2:8–9 (NIV): "For it is by grace you have been saved, through faith—and this not from yourselves, it is the gift of God - not by works, so that no one can boast."

You are a miracle man John and a living testimony to the power of the Holy Spirit acting in and through our lives. Give Frances a BIG hug from me and keep giving thanks for the wonderful blessings in your life. You have a rich storehouse of inner blessings that your mind, body and spirit galvanized and used in a coordinated way, and at the right time, to bring you back from the brink of death.

I am so pleased that you have put your story in print form for many to read and ponder over. For me it is a remarkable story of faith and belief in the Power of the Holy Spirit in our lives. We are strengthened as a result of such journeys and life experiences. Why some people survive as has clearly happened in your case and not others we will never know. I believe nothing

experience. Copies have also been handed to people who knew nothing about the accident, and they are equally surprised when they read some of the details. One Sunday evening at church I explained to Jim Clarke that we were handing out copies of my story, and he said, "People are giving you an opportunity to share your faith; they are in fact opening the door for you. Handing them a printed copy provides them with some details of the miracle of your survival and the horrific injuries you sustained, particularly as these are not obvious now for anyone to see." The feedback and positive comments received from many people have all helped to sow the seed for *Spared by Grace*.

More than once I was asked, "Have you ever thought about writing a book?" but this was never something I believed I was capable of. I knew it would be good to document in more detail my miraculous survival and the many answered prayers that we've experienced, but these thoughts were soon pushed aside by doubts in my ability. At times I wondered if someone else could write my story. Would they be able to express what I wanted to say? Again more doubts about the idea would creep in, and I tried to forget about the whole thing.

At the beginning of March 2016, my daughter Stephanie and her husband suggested that I download a new Bible application on my phone, and they recommended one to me by YouVersion. It was through this app two days later that I signed up to receive free daily devotionals from FaithGateway, which I began to look forward to receiving each day.

Frances first publicly shared how God had gone before her and carried her through this whole journey at a testimony service at our local church one evening in July. From then on, we have been asked many times to share our remarkable story at various church meetings. We never find this easy, but from the beginning, both Frances and I have felt it was only right when asked to share what God has taken us and our family through. We have been to ladies' guilds, men's breakfast events, various church coffee mornings, and so on. Taking with us some printed copies has proved very popular, and many people have taken them to share with friends. We continue to hope and pray that God will use these for his glory and to touch someone's life. We both shared our story at the end of July 2016 at a Sunday evening service in the AOG

Central Church in Fraserburgh. Frances and I had been there on the Sunday evening before the accident; again, this was a congregation who had witnessed a very visible answer to their many prayers. Many people said what an amazing story we had and how much it had encouraged them. My thoughts about writing a book rematerialized. I continued to pray about this and asked God for guidance, but I couldn't shake off the doubts in my own ability.

The daily devotional that I received on August 12 was entitled "Answer the call to publish your book" and offered a free publishing guide from the Christian publisher WestBow Press. This was undoubtedly more leading to write a book! I researched WestBow and was very much impressed and encouraged by their moral statements and clear publishing guidelines. These standards seemed to fit exactly with my own thoughts, and within a couple of days I had signed up for a self-publishing contract. It can sometimes be easier to see God's leading when looking back because, at the time, I had absolutely no idea where to begin with sourcing a publisher or how to even go about writing a book, and all these things only added to my doubts. I would never have discovered WestBow Press on my own, and I wouldn't have managed to complete the manuscript without their help and guidance. I have no doubt this was again clear prompting by the Holy Spirit.

The following details offer a few brief examples of the people God has unexpectedly put in our path. I attended a medical appointment at a hospital in Edinburgh, and following the appointment Frances and I were about halfway through our three-hour drive home when we stopped at a service station in Dundee for fuel. It was always better for me at the time to move a little bit whenever possible, so we went into the shop to use the toilet and to buy some coffee. As we were heading back to the car, we met a woman at the door whose father and mother had been involved in a car crash and were patients along with me in ARI. Both families had spent many hours together in the relative's room at intensive care and experienced similar ups and downs. They became friends at the time but hadn't seen each other since, other than briefly passing at the neurology clinic. We were all delighted to see one another. The conversation continued, and obvious inquiries were

made regarding everyone's health and recovery. I handed her a couple of copies of my story so she could pass them on to her parents. Some may see this as a freak coincidence, but what are the chances that we would meet their daughter in an unusual city at an unusual time as we only decided at the last minute to stop for fuel? For her to be in that service station at the same time as us was no coincidence.

Later that year in August, Frances and I were invited to a friend's daughter's wedding at a hotel on the banks of Loch Lomond. We stayed the weekend, and everyone had a great time. We met many people we hadn't seen in a long time, which we enjoyed; I handed copies of my story to many friends when they asked about the accident. As we were leaving the wedding reception on Saturday night, a woman from Peterhead who vaguely knew Frances came over to speak with us. I didn't recognize or even remember her immediately, but she was amazed to see me and went on to explain that she worked as an operating room nurse at ARI and was on duty when I was taken in for surgery at A&E. She mentioned the various surgeons who had been involved and praised their many skills and dedication, and more than once she said she was amazed at how I had recovered. She then added that I was still on the operating table when they transferred over to the night shift and that they hadn't held out much hope for me that day. I gave her a copy of my story listing the many answered prayers, hopefully explaining the reason for my survival. Along with her colleagues, she had been given a front-row seat to experience God's hand upon me and my survival, beating all odds and beyond all expectations.

The following month, Frances and I took a short trip to Belfast for two days, mainly to see the Christian singer-songwriters Keith and Kristyn Getty in concert at the Waterfront Hall, which we really enjoyed. During an interval in the program, I was standing next to gentleman in the foyer. We started a brief conversation, which s turned to the accident and my injuries. I handed him a copy of my as we parted, and he sent the following e-mail a couple of days la

Thank you John for sharing your remarkable/ amazing story with me. Yes it was good to meet you is accidental or happens by chance. You are alive for a reason and that is to quietly show the power of family and friends united purposefully in prayer and believing that healing was possible. For me the miracle was an outworking of the Holy Spirit from within.

May you never think otherwise and may Frances never lose her gracious smile. I know you won't. The story is a testimony to that strong belief you both have. I myself am going through a very difficult time at present and your story has given me heart. Thank you.

Blessings and Peace.
Wesley

The e-mail was a great encouragement to both Frances and me.

In March 2017 Frances and I were at a local hardware store in Peterhead when we noticed a fire and rescue service truck in the car park. Frances went over to hand them a copy of my story (as she does) on the off chance they might have known any of the crew who attended the accident. The driver didn't know anything about the crash, but an officer came out of the back of the truck and said he had been at the scene of the accident. He was visibly delighted to see me and said that after I left in the air ambulance, they never heard how things turned out. I was shocked at how much detail he remembered, especially considering that almost three years had now passed. He explained that, as they waited for specialized cutting equipment to arrive, he sat next to me in the passenger seat to reassure me they were doing all they could. The biggest shock came when he said that I replied to him. He seemed to remember me mumbling, "Get me out of here as quickly as you can." This came as a real surprise to me. I have no memory of the accident, but up until then I assumed I had been knocked unconscious almost immediately and remained that way for some time.

The officer went on to explain why it had taken over an hour to free me from the car. The front wheel on the driver's side was inside the car, beside me, and around my legs. When I explained that I didn't remember anything from that day, he said, "Well, I think that's just as well. It was not a pretty sight." He praised the paramedics who were on scene for their efficient and very skillful teamwork, and he remembered one of them saying as they were freeing me from the wreckage, "If we get this guy in the air ambulance and he makes it to hospital, he may have a fighting chance."

I can't remember exactly when, but sometime later that year, I attended a funeral service and sat across the aisle from a well-known Peterhead businessman with whom I hadn't spoken since before the accident. He was delighted to see me and amazed at my recovery. His words were, "It really is only by the grace of God that you are still alive." This struck a chord and planted a seed for the title *Spared by Grace*. Prior to this, I had spent months pondering an appropriate title. Many times I had asked God for guidance, but up until then I felt like I was getting nowhere.

Convince the Inconvincible

The subheading for this part was suggested by my good friend Gary Bruce, whom I have known for many years, but due to different family circumstances and changing work patterns, we lost touch with one another. We had passed each other often enough but hadn't actually spoken in possibly fifteen or twenty years. Three weeks before my accident, we unexpectedly met at an oil and gas industry safety meeting in a hotel near Aberdeen. This seminar is held a couple of times each year and is attended by many from the industry. This was the first meeting Gary had been to as he was asked last minute to cover for a colleague. We sat next to each other and enjoyed catching up with family news over lunch. Gary made the time to come and visit me every week while I was in the Ugie Hospital, and along with his lovely wife Jane, the four of us have become very good friends. I'm convinced that the way our paths unexpectedly crossed at this meeting was no coincidence, and since my discharge from the hospital the four of us have met up frequently and developed a strong friendship. We meet every few weeks for lunch, and Frances and I have shared many details of our experience with them, in particular the many answered prayers we've seen.

experience. Copies have also been handed to people who knew nothing about the accident, and they are equally surprised when they read some of the details. One Sunday evening at church I explained to Jim Clarke that we were handing out copies of my story, and he said, "People are giving you an opportunity to share your faith; they are in fact opening the door for you. Handing them a printed copy provides them with some details of the miracle of your survival and the horrific injuries you sustained, particularly as these are not obvious now for anyone to see." The feedback and positive comments received from many people have all helped to sow the seed for *Spared by Grace.*

More than once I was asked, "Have you ever thought about writing a book?" but this was never something I believed I was capable of. I knew it would be good to document in more detail my miraculous survival and the many answered prayers that we've experienced, but these thoughts were soon pushed aside by doubts in my ability. At times I wondered if someone else could write my story. Would they be able to express what I wanted to say? Again more doubts about the idea would creep in, and I tried to forget about the whole thing.

At the beginning of March 2016, my daughter Stephanie and her husband suggested that I download a new Bible application on my phone, and they recommended one to me by YouVersion. It was through this app two days later that I signed up to receive free daily devotionals from FaithGateway, which I began to look forward to receiving each day.

Frances first publicly shared how God had gone before her and carried her through this whole journey at a testimony service at our local church one evening in July. From then on, we have been asked many times to share our remarkable story at various church meetings. We never find this easy, but from the beginning, both Frances and I have felt it was only right when asked to share what God has taken us and our family through. We have been to ladies' guilds, men's breakfast events, various church coffee mornings, and so on. Taking with us some printed copies has proved very popular, and many people have taken them to share with friends. We continue to hope and pray that God will use these for his glory and to touch someone's life. We both shared our story at the end of July 2016 at a Sunday evening service in the AOG

Central Church in Fraserburgh. Frances and I had been there on the Sunday evening before the accident; again, this was a congregation who had witnessed a very visible answer to their many prayers. Many people said what an amazing story we had and how much it had encouraged them. My thoughts about writing a book rematerialized. I continued to pray about this and asked God for guidance, but I couldn't shake off the doubts in my own ability.

The daily devotional that I received on August 12 was entitled "Answer the call to publish your book" and offered a free publishing guide from the Christian publisher WestBow Press. This was undoubtedly more leading to write a book! I researched WestBow and was very much impressed and encouraged by their moral statements and clear publishing guidelines. These standards seemed to fit exactly with my own thoughts, and within a couple of days I had signed up for a self-publishing contract. It can sometimes be easier to see God's leading when looking back because, at the time, I had absolutely no idea where to begin with sourcing a publisher or how to even go about writing a book, and all these things only added to my doubts. I would never have discovered WestBow Press on my own, and I wouldn't have managed to complete the manuscript without their help and guidance. I have no doubt this was again clear prompting by the Holy Spirit.

The following details offer a few brief examples of the people God has unexpectedly put in our path. I attended a medical appointment at a hospital in Edinburgh, and following the appointment Frances and I were about halfway through our three-hour drive home when we stopped at a service station in Dundee for fuel. It was always better for me at the time to move a little bit whenever possible, so we went into the shop to use the toilet and to buy some coffee. As we were heading back to the car, we met a woman at the door whose father and mother had been involved in a car crash and were patients along with me in ARI. Both families had spent many hours together in the relative's room at intensive care and experienced similar ups and downs. They became friends at the time but hadn't seen each other since, other than briefly passing at the neurology clinic. We were all delighted to see one another. The conversation continued, and obvious inquiries were made regarding everyone's health and recovery. I handed her a couple of copies of my story so she could pass them on to her parents. Some may see this as a freak coincidence, but what are the chances that we would meet their daughter in an unusual city at an unusual time as we only decided at the last minute to stop for fuel? For her to be in that service station at the same time as us was no coincidence.

Later that year in August, Frances and I were invited to a friend's daughter's wedding at a hotel on the banks of Loch Lomond. We stayed the weekend, and everyone had a great time. We met many people we hadn't seen in a long time, which we enjoyed; I handed copies of my story to many friends when they asked about the accident. As we were leaving the wedding reception on Saturday night, a woman from Peterhead who vaguely knew Frances came over to speak with us. I didn't recognize or even remember her immediately, but she was amazed to see me and went on to explain that she worked as an operating room nurse at ARI and was on duty when I was taken in for surgery at A&E. She mentioned the various surgeons who had been involved and praised their many skills and dedication, and more than once she said she was amazed at how I had recovered. She then added that I was still on the operating table when they transferred over to the night shift and that they hadn't held out much hope for me that day. I gave her a copy of my story listing the many answered prayers, hopefully explaining the reason for my survival. Along with her colleagues, she had been given a front-row seat to experience God's hand upon me and my survival, beating all odds and beyond all expectations.

The following month, Frances and I took a short trip to Belfast for two days, mainly to see the Christian singer-songwriters Keith and Kristyn Getty in concert at the Waterfront Hall, which we really enjoyed. During an interval in the program, I was standing next to a gentleman in the foyer. We started a brief conversation, which soon turned to the accident and my injuries. I handed him a copy of my story as we parted, and he sent the following e-mail a couple of days later.

Thank you John for sharing your remarkable/ amazing story with me. Yes it was good to meet you

at the Waterfront Hall on Thursday evening and meet
your lovely wife Frances whose wonderful smile told
me everything and why you are still standing. You
had EVERYTHING to live for, and deep down your
subconscious knew that. A lovely wife, three great
children, a faith that was strong and empowering,
and a community of friends (church and wider
family) who believed you could be healed. As the
quote says … 'the directions are always within'. The
Holy Spirit was at work in your life John and you are
a living testimony of that.

We are all here for a purpose and your purpose
now is to meet with people and let them know in your
own quiet and modest way that you were 'saved' for
a purpose. Your remarkable story will cause people
to think and ask questions about the meaning of life.
Our savior lives. Ephesians 2:8–9 (NIV): "For it is
by grace you have been saved, through faith—and
this not from yourselves, it is the gift of God - not by
works, so that no one can boast."

You are a miracle man John and a living testimony
to the power of the Holy Spirit acting in and through
our lives. Give Frances a BIG hug from me and keep
giving thanks for the wonderful blessings in your
life. You have a rich storehouse of inner blessings that
your mind, body and spirit galvanized and used in a
coordinated way, and at the right time, to bring you
back from the brink of death.

I am so pleased that you have put your story in
print form for many to read and ponder over. For me it
is a remarkable story of faith and belief in the Power of
the Holy Spirit in our lives. We are strengthened as a
result of such journeys and life experiences. Why some
people survive as has clearly happened in your case
and not others we will never know. I believe nothing

Gary has stated more than once that this whole journey we've been on has convinced him (the "inconvincible," in his own words) of the awesome power of prayer. Gary made a commitment to the Lord many years before but had drifted somewhat from his faith, but the Lord never leaves those who believe in him. Another detail Gary shared with me recently was how he prayed for the first time in many years when he heard about my accident and made up his mind that if I survived and pulled through, he would go back to church. He attended my baptism service with his wife and thought he had fulfilled his obligation; however, he has been drawn back to church, much to Jane's delight, and they enjoy attending almost every week.

> Now I want you to know, brothers, that what has happened to me has really served to advance the gospel. (Philippians 1:12 NIV)

Their eldest daughter Eilidh recently graduated with a degree in medicine, causing me to reflect on the first time she sat next to me in church. Following the service we discussed some details of my injuries and recovery, and she frequently asked how this was or how was that. Gary told me later that Eilidh knew about all my injuries as she had read my story. When Gary asked her what she thought about my recovery, she said it was truly amazing, but the biggest surprise to her was that I was fine. On another night we went to their house when Eilidh and her boyfriend Chris (who is also a doctor) were there. I was asked to take a copy of my X-rays along, and they studied them for most of the evening. They were both able to point out and explain many details that we knew nothing about and were truly amazed at what they saw, saying it reminded them of the type of situation they would have been shown in an exam as the worst possible scenario and asked to give a prognosis and explain how to deal with the situation.

Although they come less frequently now, we still continue to be surprised at the unexpected opportunities we are given to hand people a copy of my remarkable story.

chapter 13

Family, a Great Blessing!

Give thanks to the Lord, for he is good; his love endures forever.
—Psalm 118:1 (NIV)

… But as for me and my household, we will serve the Lord.
—Joshua 24:15 (NIV)

Blessed is the man who perseveres under trial, because
when he has stood the test, he will receive the crown of
life that God has promised to those who love him.
—James 1:12 (NIV)

I HAVE BEEN blessed with a wonderful family, and in this chapter, they describe some of their experiences before, during, and after the car crash, as well as how they have also been part of this remarkable journey.

My family today

Frances

> But this happened that we might not rely on ourselves
> but on God, who raises the dead. He has delivered us
> from such a deadly peril, and he will deliver us again.
> On him we have set our hope that he will continue
> to deliver us, as you help us by your prayers. Then
> many will give thanks on our behalf for the gracious
> favor granted us in answer to the prayers of many. (2
> Corinthians 1:9–11 NIV)

God has indeed delivered us in answer to the prayers of many! On
him we have set our hope. If I were to sum up the last few years, it
would have to be in these three verses:

…apart from me you can do nothing. (John 15:5 NIV)

Look to the Lord and his strength, seek his face always. (Psalm 105:5 NIV)

All things are possible with God. (Mark 10:27 NIV)

God has been so faithful. I've been a Christian for over forty-five years, and although I've let the Lord down many, many times, he's never let me down. He's never left me.

> The Lord himself goes before you and will be with you; he will never leave you nor forsake you. Do not be afraid; do not be discouraged.
> (Deuteronomy 31:8 NIV)

That is so true; God in his grace and in his faithfulness went before me at the time of John's accident. All the scripture I read in the days and weeks leading up to the accident encouraged me and reminded me that nothing is impossible with God. Life was so busy just before John's accident, and the week of the accident I remember thinking I had a really busy week ahead, but none of it seemed important as I sat next to John in intensive care. I couldn't even remember what I was supposed to be busy with!

Reverend Abi Ngunga once said, "If you have nothing but you have Jesus Christ as your Savior, you have everything. If you have everything, but you don't have Jesus Christ as your Savior, you have nothing."

This was very real in intensive care. When John squeezed my hand, I remember thinking it was worth a million pounds. I also thought that even if I gave a million pounds, it couldn't make John live. John's life was very much in God's hands, and that was a great comfort. God was in control, and he knew the bigger picture. His ways are higher than ours, and his way is perfect.

As for God, his way is perfect: The Lord's word is flawless; he shields all who take refuge in him. (Psalm 18:30 NIV)

"For my thoughts are not your thoughts, neither are you ways my ways," declares the Lord. "As the heavens are higher than the earth, so are my ways higher than your ways and my thoughts than your thoughts." (Isaiah 55:8–9 NIV)

God not only had John in his hands; he had all of us in his hands too. Without Christ there is no hope, but with Christ there is great hope no matter what happens. John knew Jesus as his Lord and Savior, so I had hope that even if he died, I would see him again in heaven.

Jesus said to her, "I am the resurrection and the life. He who believes in me will live, even though he dies; and whoever lives and believes in me will never die. Do you believe this?" (John 11:25–26 NIV)

Then Jesus said, "Did I not tell you that if you believed you would see the glory of God?" (John 11:40 NIV)

What comfort those verses bring when life is hanging by a thread! I could do nothing for myself and clung to the Lord. God was so close; he really was my shield and refuge.

When I wasn't with John, I spent every minute I could reading my Bible and praying. It filled me with hope because it took my eyes off the difficulties around me and put them on to God, who is sovereign, who had John and our whole family in his hands, whose way is perfect, and who can do all things. It reminded me that God can do more than all we could ask or imagine and that nothing in all creation can separate us from his love, not even death itself.

It was a great comfort and encouragement to be part of God's family and to know that people were praying. The cards, text messages, and practical help we received from everyone were such an encouragement and came just when we needed it most. They were a great blessing to us, and we are so thankful to those who took the time to pray, help, and encourage us in so many ways. To *encourage* means "to put courage in." All those folks certainly encouraged us; they put the courage in.

I thought people might stop praying for John when he moved to an ordinary ward, but even today there are people who pray every day for John. They are such an example and encouragement. I once read somewhere, "Feed your faith, and your fears will starve to death." Focusing on God and his promises filled us with hope. Focusing on the problems and circumstances fed our fears.

When John moved to the orthopedic ward on Monday, July 6, the fear that people might stop praying for him grew. John's confusion seemed worse; I wasn't sure he knew I was his wife. He knew my name was Frances, but his speech was so different—it was formal and full of big words. He didn't know how to do simple things, such as pressing the bell to call for the nurse, and after he learned how to, he buzzed all the time for no reason. He didn't know where he was, and instead of focusing on God, I started to look at the problems and circumstances. My fears grew.

One Wednesday morning, Ann Bowlerwell from church phoned. I can't remember what I said, but I remember Ann saying, "Cast not away thy confidence." It was just what I needed to hear. She reminded me that our confidence is in God.

> So do not throw away your confidence; it will be richly rewarded.
> (Hebrews 10:35 NIV)

Many prayer requests went out, and as I could do nothing for myself, I prayed about everything—strength for the day, parking spaces, wheelchairs, our coming and going, visitors, wisdom for the medical staff, the clinics. I was so weak that I really couldn't think about things for myself and had to hand them all to God, even things we usually take for granted.

Every morning I read Isaiah 40:28–31 (NIV).
Do you not know?
Have you not heard?
The Lord is the everlasting God,
the Creator of the ends of the earth.
He will not grow tired or weary,
and his understanding no one can fathom.
He gives strength to the weary
and increases the power of the weak.
Even youths grow tired and weary,
and young men stumble and fall;
But those who hope in the Lord
will renew their strength.
They will soar on wings like eagles;
they will run and not grow weary,
they will walk and not be faint.

God met our every need! We have seen many, many answers to prayer, more than I could write down. John really is a Peterhead miracle.

Many, O Lord my God, are the wonders you have done. The things you planned for us no one can recount to you; were I to speak and tell of them, they would be too many to declare. (Ps. 40:5 NIV)

Strength for today and bright hope for tomorrow,
Blessings all mine with ten thousand besides.
Great is Thy faithfulness! Great is Thy faithfulness
Morning by morning new mercies I see.
All I have needed Thy hand hath provided
Great is Thy faithfulness Lord unto me!
—Thomas O Chisholm

I want to encourage you as I have been encouraged; God is bigger than any problem you are facing. God is a God of miracles. He hears and answers prayer! Nothing is impossible for God. There is no problem too small for God either; he cares about every detail, and he knows every hair on your head. His love for us reaches to the heavens and his faithfulness to the skies. If Jesus is your Savior, you are never without hope no matter what happens. Nothing in all creation can separate you from his love (see Romans 8). If Jesus is your Savior, then God is your Father and you are part of his worldwide family. If Jesus is your Savior, the same power that raised him from the dead is at work in you. If you don't know Jesus as your Savior, the good news is that he died for you too and he will be your Savior if you ask him to forgive your sins and come into your heart. You can have the same hope, the same peace. God promises never to leave us or forsake us.

Monica

> The Lord himself goes before you and will be with you; he will never leave you nor forsake you. Do not be afraid; do not be discouraged.
> (Deuteronomy 31:8 NIV)

> God is our refuge and strength, an ever-present help in trouble.
> (Psalm 46:1 NIV)

The scripture above tells us that God goes before us. In January 2014, almost six months before John's accident, I believe God was doing exactly that.

I had been spending some time praying and reading my Bible as I do most mornings, but as I prayed with my eyes closed, I began to have the sensation of being in a car and having a sudden realization that there was another car heading straight toward me. The thought immediately came into my mind, *There's going to be a head-on collision.* I then saw a picture in my mind of a twisted, mangled, piece of metal. I knew it was the remains of a car after this accident, but I couldn't distinguish what kind of car it was or whose it was.

The sensation and the image were so incredibly vivid that it shocked me. After a few minutes of processing what I had seen and felt, I began to pray again. I said, "Lord, what was that? I do believe this was from You, but what are you showing me? Is this about to happen to me or to Zander (my husband)?" Even as I prayed, I was thinking, *That's a very negative thing to pray about.* As I prayed, though, I felt an incredible peace, and a picture came into my mind of us both (God, I believe, showing me something good that will happen in the future), and we were both mobile and clearly alive.

The image of the mangled car stayed with me for quite some time and would often come into my mind in the coming months. I did sense God was preparing me for something that was about to happen, and each time I was reminded about it, as I prayed, I always got the sense that God was asking me just to trust him with it—whatever it meant—and to continue to pray about it.

The day after John's accident, when I saw the images of his car on the news reports and in the newspaper, they were exactly what I had seen as I prayed. The twisted, mangled metal that God had shown me almost six months before had been John's car. Even in the anguish and the heartbreak of that first day after the accident, there was something so reassuring and comforting to know that God had revealed beforehand that this would happen. It brought a reassurance that he was still very much in control; that even though this was an incredible shock to us, it wasn't a shock to him. He knew it was about to happen and was an ever-present help in this time of trouble. As I looked at those images of John's car and connected them with what God had shown me, I also sensed God saying that John was going to be all right—that as critical as he was at that moment, he was going to live.

Stephanie and Michael

Stephanie and Michael were married only two weeks before the car crash and had just returned home from their honeymoon when the accident took place. This was a very stormy and challenging start to their marriage, but their strong faith and trust in God has carried them through many more ups and downs since their wedding day. The following paragraphs will detail some of these. Their son, Michael Jr., was born on October 27, 2015, and was a cause for great celebration. The joy of being blessed with grandchildren is a great privilege, and Frances and I are truly thankful. Michael worked in the oil and gas industry as a surveyor for the American Bureau of Shipping (ABS) and was based in the Aberdeen office. Part of his contract required him to undergo an annual medical examination; this is standard practice in the industry and gave no reason for concern as he was a fit and healthy twenty-two-year-old man.

A small irregularity in his kidney function was detected through a blood test, and he was advised this should be monitored as his kidney function may deteriorate further later in life. His general practitioner was informed and referred him to a specialist as a precautionary measure, with the result that his kidney function would now be monitored periodically. Several months later, Michael was made redundant during the oil and gas industry downturn in 2016, but he quickly found employment at Peterhead Harbour. This new job was manual work, helping discharge the catch from a number of fishing vessels. There are no regular hours in this type of work, but he enjoyed the flexibility and settled into his new occupation. Routine blood tests were taken and again indicated a further reduction in his kidney function much sooner than anticipated, which would require more frequent monitoring. This came as a shock to everyone but was particularly difficult for his wife with their one-year-old son. Subsequent tests showed that his kidneys were continuing to deteriorate quite drastically, with his levels recorded at 11 percent on February 10, 2017, and he began to feel quite unwell. He was forced to give up work. Various options were discussed with his consultant, a kidney transplant being the most effective long-term solution. When this news became common knowledge, many of his friends and relatives offered to donate a kidney, which to Michael was a truly humbling experience.

Shortly after his diagnosis, both of Michael's parents and his older brother, John Duncan, began a series of tests to determine their suitability as potential donors. It was also decided to add Michael to the National Health Service (NHS) transplant list, but in reality his family members were his best prospects, as the average time spent on the NHS list before a suitable organ became available was three years. Suitability tests continued with Michael's parents and both were a good match, and the decision was made to proceed with Michael's dad as the selected donor. At the same time, his kidney disease worsened and peritoneal dialysis commenced at home on April 10. This continued four times each day, and his health began to improve slightly although he was constantly exhausted and slept for long periods of each day. Throughout this time, many people were praying for Michael and his family, asking God for his full recovery and complete healing. Stephanie and Michael regularly attend Apex Church in Peterhead and have many Christian friends there. Family members from both sides are also well known in various different churches, and it was always a great comfort to know that so many people were praying for Michael. Around mid-May 2017, the leaders from Apex Church came one night to their home in order to pray over Michael. I would say this was probably when his condition was at its worst and he was very ill.

Over the following week or two, his condition slowly improved again and he began to feel a little stronger. My family and I were invited to their house on Tuesday, May 30, for a meal to celebrate my fifty-first birthday. This went very well, everyone enjoyed the evening, and it was great to see Michael feeling a little better. At one thirty the following morning, we were suddenly awakened when Frances's phone began to ring. Our first reaction and thought was that something must be wrong. It was Stephanie calling to say they had just received an unexpected call from the hospital to say that a potential kidney was available, and they would like Michael to come to Edinburgh Royal Infirmary as soon as possible. Everything was arranged quickly. Frances went to their house to babysit Michael Jr., and Michael's parents drove them straight to Edinburgh. When they arrived at the hospital, Michael was quickly taken for tests, the results of which were all satisfactory, so surgery could go ahead as soon as possible. Before he went to the operating room, the surgeon said he had never seen a more suitable match and that, if he were in Michael's shoes, he would be happy. The total function of Michael's kidneys was recorded before he went in for surgery—it had dropped to a staggering 6 percent.

Everything went well in surgery, and a successful kidney transplant was completed. This was a huge relief for everyone, and again many prayers were answered. Almost immediately, his new kidney started working normally, and its function was recorded at between 40 percent and 50 percent. This is truly remarkable. Michael remained in the hospital for ten days as the doctors closely monitored his condition and regulated his antirejection drugs. Rejection is a common complication with transplant surgery, where Michael's own immune system would detect the foreign kidney and act to try to destroy it. He will continue to take immunosuppressant medication for the rest of his life, which leaves him more prone to infections than the average person, and he has to be very careful to avoid even the most trivial illness, such as the common cold.

Stephanie takes part in a ladies daily devotional group, and she posted the following in July 2017.

This was my prayer over 2017: "He must become greater, I must become less."

Ephesians 3:20 (NIV): "Now to him who is able to do immeasurably more than all we could ask or imagine, according to his power that is at work in us."

There's lots of time left in 2017, and God has already answered my prayer but not how I expected.

February began and with it I had to face the fact that "till death do us part" could be fifty years sooner than I anticipated. Our income stopped and even with the best possible medical outcome I'd have to forget about having any more children—my husband, Michael, was in the final stage of kidney failure. "(Love) … bears all things, believes all things, hopes all things, endures all things. Love never fails" (1 Corinthians 13:7–8 (NKJV).

The verses about love in 1 Corinthians 13 are the ones that were read at my wedding, and although I'd heard these verses lots of times before, God really implanted them on my heart that day and they've been very special to me ever since, popping to the front of my mind every now and again. I wish I could say that my love was enough to bear and endure through this season, constantly believing and hoping, however it wasn't. At times it really was hard to speak faith into my fear of what the future held and how Michael and I's life together could completely change.

> And so we know and rely on the love God has for us…
> Perfect love casts out all fear. (1 John 4:16, 18 NIV)

God's love for me on the other hand is so different! Relying on and praising God for his love gave me the strength to bear and endure circumstances I didn't ever imagine I'd have to face. God's perfect love for me helps me believe the promises he's given me, which gives me hope in situations that seem hopeless. It's in the moments of complete surrender of myself and my family to God's plan have I felt most strengthened and loved by him.

He has made everything beautiful in its time. (Ecclesiastes 3:11 NIV)

I think when we surrender ourselves and our situations to God, he magnifies himself in our hearts and minds, making us more like him—more beautiful. Just like a little seed planted in dark, ugly soil, it sometimes takes a season that seems dark and ugly to help us grow more beautiful like our Lord Jesus.

God has been more than faithful to us as a family, and I'm completely humbled and thankful that Michael is doing really well with a miraculous kidney transplant—and I'm twenty-two weeks pregnant!

God is so good, and his plans for us are always good. I believe when we submit ourselves, our plans, our futures, and our families to God—making ourselves less—he becomes greater in our lives and his love, power, beauty, and peace are magnified in us.

What a wonderful way to announce her pregnancy. My second grandchild, Emma, arrived safely on December 1, 2017.

One evening in September 2018, my sister Grace and her family were at our house for a meal. The subject of *Spared by Grace* came up, and during the conversation that followed I was made aware for the first time that my nephew Alexander had been on his way to work in Aberdeen on the day of the accident. He had also been in the daily line of cars in the morning commute and was around seven or eight cars behind me when the accident took place. The traffic in front of him started to brake hard and came to a complete stop, Alexander couldn't see why but then noticed that a lorry up ahead heading in the opposite direction also stopped, and he suspected something had taken place up ahead on the road. When the two cars in front started to turn around and head back in the opposite direction, Alexander assumed they had seen something and did the same. A few seconds later he was passed by several emergency service vehicles rushing to the scene, confirming his suspicions that something serious had taken place. He had no idea how bad it was or who was involved until he arrived at work and the news had started to filter through. It is remarkable really that, had he been a few meters further ahead, he may have witnessed the whole incident. I'm sure it was God's hand on the whole situation that ensured Alexander was prevented from witnessing any more than he did.

chapter 14

Reflection

Be still, and know that I am God;
I will be exalted among the nations,
I will be exalted in the earth.

—Psalm 46:10 (NIV)

Do good to your servant according to your word, O Lord.
Teach me knowledge and good judgement, for I believe in your commands.
Before I was afflicted I went astray, but now I obey your word.
You are good, and what you do is good; teach me your decrees.
Though the arrogant have smeared me with lies,
I keep your precepts with all my heart.
Their hearts are callous and unfeeling, but I delight in your law.
It was good for me to be afflicted so that I might learn your decrees.
The law from your mouth is more precious to me
than thousands of pieces of silver and gold.

—Psalm 119: 65–72 (NIV)

No one can believe how powerful prayer is and what it can
effect, except those who have learned it by experience.

—Martin Luther

THE PSALM READS, "Be still, and know that I am God," but the fast pace of modern life can easily prevent us from appreciating this. Through the course of my recovery, but in particular while working on the manuscript for *Spared by Grace*, I have spent many hours being still. It has been mostly during these times that I have reflected not only on my brush with death but on my life in general. There have been a few details that I've struggled to remember, and others that are completely new to me. It would have been impossible to record these without the help and guidance of my wife and family. We have spent many hours looking back over the events, sometimes laughing and joking as we shared different perspectives. While attempting to bring *Spared by Grace* to a close, I struggle to find the words to adequately express how thankful I am to be alive. Repeatedly I have pondered over the question, "Why was my life spared?"

The late evangelist Billy Graham wrote in his book *Nearing Home* that "Christians are not to be preoccupied with death; God has put within each of us a will to survive. But neither are we to shrink from death or act as though we must fiercely resist it until the last breath." This entire journey has made the inevitability of death very real to me, much more than ever before. Life now has a very different meaning; every breath we take is a very simple yet profound privilege, and anyone who's been carried through a near-death experience can perhaps relate to this. Most of us will experience the sadness of death at some point through the loss of a close relative or loved one, but none of us knows when our own lives on earth will end. This is something we have absolutely no control over. I'm left with a strange feeling after this whole journey that I find difficult to explain, and this may be the result of having no memory of the accident or anything that happened that day. I have no shocking or horrific images ingrained in my mind from seeing the other car cross the road and realizing the inevitability of what was to come. I did not see my life flash before my eyes as is sometimes described at these moments, nor did I experience a small glimpse of heaven as some people may have done. I'm sure the effects of the brain injury I sustained contributed to the gaps left in my memory, as the symptoms I experience come as no surprise to the medical profession.

But I still find it amazing how the brain has the ability to completely erase traumatic events from memory. In my own case I see this as a great blessing; some people who have experienced similar traumatic injuries say the flashbacks more than the injuries are often the most difficult things to overcome and can take many months, even years in some cases.

We read in the book of Ecclesiastes 7:2 (NIV), "For death is the destiny of every man, the living should take this to heart." The Bible states very clearly that we will all spend eternity in either heaven or hell! There is no "nothing after life," and we are all given the freedom to choose. People can be deceived into thinking they have plenty of time and that they can choose heaven later. The only real certainty is that the decision is required in advance, as death can come in an instant—at the blink of an eye, as they say. This may seem like a simple and obvious statement to make; however, the car crash has made this very real to me and is something we can all take for granted. I left for work on a beautiful summer morning, everything seemed fine, and I felt in good health. According to eyewitness reports, I was driving normally when a car traveling in the opposite direction crossed the road for no apparent reason and hit me head on. Life can indeed change in a split second!

It has often been said that I was lucky, and some people may question my claim that God spared my life, particularly as many people die from serious traffic accidents every day. Why did I survive? Why me? I have frequently asked myself these questions. Was it a miracle that I survived the head-on collision—particularly as almost everyone who saw me that day was surprised I was alive? The paramedic who was first to arrive at the accident gave me a "1 percent chance of being removed from the vehicle alive." My GCS was recorded at 5, and it took the emergency services over an hour to cut me free of the car as the front wheel on the driver's side was inside the car around my legs. He said I was "completely trapped," and as he sat behind me holding my head as the roof was removed, concerns grew for his own safety as the vehicle was slowly filling up with smoke and oil. He described the car as effectively sitting on top of me and explained that in situations like these, toxins produced from the numerous injuries and damaged, crushed, and dying tissues normally rush to the heart when the casualty is released, resulting in death—a situation he had seen before at similar scenes. It was said, "If we get this guy in the air ambulance alive and he makes it to hospital, he may have a fighting chance."

What about the availability of the air ambulance? It was scrambled from Inverness and landed at the scene around twenty to twenty-five minutes later. The equipment was ready and in place before I was cut from the car, and it took eight minutes to fly me to the hospital. Or was it that the team of surgeons who specialized in the treatment I needed was available at ARI when I was admitted? So many pieces of the puzzle just seemed to come together at the right time for me to survive. God uses all these things to carry out his will.

This may be seen as lucky by some and no more than a series of fortunate coincidences. A pastor jokingly remarked one day that people who don't believe in God would say that I was so lucky, I should try the lottery. What about the fact that throughout the whole experience of the accident, surgery, recovery, and then further surgery, all followed by extensive physiotherapy, I've never experienced any pain? Initially I was sedated, and then I unexpectedly remained in a coma for almost two weeks; it would be easy to assume this might explain why I don't remember any pain. But daily entries in my medical records confirm this as being the case. In intensive care, statements like "Patient doesn't appear to be in any pain" were frequently made. I asked a doctor once if these entries would have been a nurse's opinion, but she said they would have known for sure as there are monitors in place to record these levels. Similar entries were made in my records from the orthopedic trauma ward. I was communicating by this time, as records regularly state, "Patient continues to deny any pain." This truly is remarkable!

What about the numerous answered prayers? Are these also no more than coincidences? Was I just very fortunate to have survived the car crash? What about my remarkable recovery? Every consultant and expert I've seen has been amazed at my recovery.

> He performs wonders that cannot be fathomed,
> miracles that cannot be counted. (Job 5:9 NIV)

I have indeed been *Spared by Grace*. As the words in the famous hymn say, it really is "amazing grace."

Personally, I don't believe in luck. God is in control of all things, and everything is ultimately worked out for his purpose for those who put their trust in him. None of us can explain why or give any clear reasons for the many challenging and difficult circumstances we all face. Events occur for which we have no human explanation. Take the car crash as a very simple example; if I were "lucky," as they say, would the other car not have just missed mine? I made this exact comment to a gentleman once, and he replied, 'Oh, then you would have been even luckier." What if I had left the house a few seconds either before or after I did? Or what if something else, or even something else? It's impossible to know on this side of eternity why my life was spared; it may have been for no other reason than to write this book and share my story. I trust that in doing so, I have demonstrated what God in his ultimate power and authority has taken me and my family through.

Many times Frances and I have been asked by various church groups to share our amazing story. After we have, people have repeatedly said to Frances, "Oh, you must have great faith," and yes, this is very evident for all to see. But Frances would rather say, "It's not so much having great faith, but having faith in a great God."

The subject of my accident and recovery came up one evening at a men's midweek Bible study. It comes up frequently, but one night a close friend asked the question, "John if you could, would you turn the clock back to before your accident and change the situation you're in?" You may think this was a strange question for a friend to ask given the circumstances, but I suspect he knew the answer. I can honestly say that I wouldn't change anything; I feel so much closer to God and now experience so much more of his peace. I've been given a completely different perspective on life; of course I wouldn't wish anyone else to go through this experience, in particular the difficulties and challenges my family faced. I still find it remarkable when I hear of the strength they were given, especially to begin with. They faced many days of uncertainty as my life was hanging by a mere thread while I was in a coma for almost two weeks with no clear or positive prognosis. They will, however, be first to tell you they had nothing or no one to cling to but God. We find it difficult to put into words how God has carried us all through, but the following verses summarize everything.

> Don't worry about anything; instead, pray about everything; tell God your needs and don't forget to thank him for his answers. If you do this you will experience God's peace which is far more wonderful than the human mind can understand. His peace will keep your thoughts and your hearts quiet and at rest as you trust in Christ Jesus.
> (Philippians 4:6–7 TLB)

My prayer throughout this remarkable journey is that whoever reads my story will be encouraged and find hope in recognizing the power and sovereignty of God in all things. The Bible states clearly that we will face many challenges and trials throughout our lives and that those of us who have accepted Jesus Christ as Lord are not immune from them. But we have the assurance that God in his mighty power and grace will help us through them, and if we trust him and truly ask for his help, we can experience the peace (real peace) that only he can provide.

Epilogue

In this you greatly rejoice, though now for a little while you may
have had to suffer grief in all kinds of trials. These have come so
that your faith—of greater worth than gold, which perishes even
though refined by fire—may be proved genuine and may result
in praise, glory and honour when Jesus Christ is revealed.

—1 Peter 1:6, 7 (NIV)

There were many days over the past three years when I thought *Spared
by Grace* would never be finished. To begin with, I could spend no more
than thirty minutes on the project every few days, and even this was
a huge effort. I quickly grew tired and weary and often thought the
whole thing was beyond me. Several weeks sometimes passed before
I looked at the manuscript again; many times it would have been far
easier just to give up. I continued to pray for strength and guidance to
finish the task. I was discussing this with a friend once who said, "I can
understand how difficult it must be reliving this whole journey as you
record the details," but I can honestly say this has not been the case,
very likely because I have no memory of the incident. I'm sure writing
the manuscript for *Spared by Grace* would have been impossible had I
remembered some of the traumatic details.

I have been convinced for some time that it was God's will for
me to complete the manuscript, but this didn't make it any easier.
Hopefully I have adequately shared some of the amazing things he
has taken me through, and I am very grateful to have been given the
strength to see it through.

I can do all things through Christ who strengthens me. (Philippians 4:13 NIV)

... and your strength will equal your days. (Deuteronomy 33:25 NIV)

List of Abbreviations

A&E—Accident and Emergency

ABS—American Bureau of Shipping

AOG—Assemblies of God

ARI—Aberdeen Royal Infirmary

CT Scan—Computerized Tomography Scan

DVLA—Driver and Vehicle Licensing Agency

GCS—Glasgow Coma Scale

GNT—Good News Translation

GP—General practitioner

ITU—Intensive Therapy Unit

MARS—Mobility and Rehabilitation Service

NIV—New International Version

NKJV—New King James Version

SMART—Southeast Mobility and Rehabilitation Technology

TLB—The Living Bible